Career Skills

Opening Doors into the Job Market

www.skills4study.com – the leading study skills website

Palgrave Study Skills

Pocket Study Skills
Series Editor: Kate Williams

Career Skills
Opening Doors into the Job Market

David Littleford
John Halstead
Charles Mulraine

palgrave
macmillan

First published 2004 by
PALGRAVE MACMILLAN

Palgrave Macmillan in the UK is an imprint of Macmillan Publishers Limited, registered in England, company number 785998, of Houndmills, Basingstoke, Hampshire RG21 6XS.

Palgrave Macmillan in the US is a division of St Martin's Press LLC, 175 Fifth Avenue, New York, NY 10010.

Palgrave Macmillan is the global academic imprint of the above companies and has companies and representatives throughout the world.

Palgrave® and Macmillan® are registered trademarks in the United States, the United Kingdom, Europe and other countries.

ISBN 978-1-4039-3627-1 paperback

This book is printed on paper suitable for recycling and made from fully managed and sustained forest sources. Logging, pulping and manufacturing processes are expected to conform to the environmental regulations of the country of origin.

A catalogue record for this book is available from the British Library.

A catalog record for this book is available from the Library of Congress.

Printed in Great Britain by the MPG Books Group, Bodmin and King's Lynn

Career Skills

Opening Doors into the Job Market

The route map below takes you through a step-by-step process from education into employment

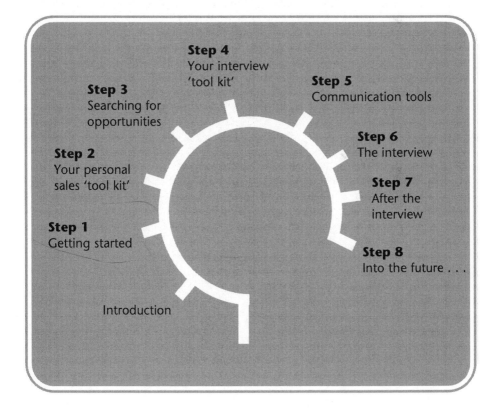

Step 4
Your interview 'tool kit'

Step 3
Searching for opportunities

Step 5
Communication tools

Step 2
Your personal sales 'tool kit'

Step 6
The interview

Step 7
After the interview

Step 1
Getting started

Step 8
Into the future . . .

Introduction

The way to get started is to quit talking and start doing.

Walt Disney (1901–66)

Contents

List of figures

Foreword

There has long been a need for a practical and easily accessible guide to the all-important transition from the world of education to the world of work. This book fills that gap. Guidance is needed, because the educational world is structured, the pathways within it are clearly signed and there are members of staff to whom to turn. Once school or college is left behind, individuals find themselves in charge of their own futures and facing a complex and largely unknown world.

There are immediate questions to be answered. What is it that I really want to do? How do I go about getting the kind of job I am looking for and what is it that is going to be expected of me, if I get it? Here is where the layout of this book is so helpful, because it deals with all these points in an orderly and sequential way. It takes job-seekers through the steps which they need to follow in order to make the most of their aims and abilities. It does so while providing realistic advice on how to approach each stage. Most usefully, it looks at all these issues from the point of view of those responsible for recruitment. Thus those who follow the book's guidance will have some idea of how to find their way to the interview stage and what to expect when they reach it.

In my view, *Career Skills: Opening Doors into the Job Market* meets the tests against which I would measure a guide of this kind. It is complete, in the sense that it covers all the necessary issues. It is universal in its approach and so it is relevant to anyone embarking on a career, whatever its nature. It is accessible, thanks to the clarity of its writing and presentation. It is also permanent. It can provide a continuing record of progress and achievement, for as long as it is kept up to date.

Perhaps its greatest strength is that, used well, it will build the confidence of its readers in themselves. Although the guidelines stress the need to be realistic about capacities and aspirations, they also emphasize the need for job-seekers not to sell themselves short. Diffidence in candidates is a more attractive trait than its opposite, but those entering employment need to be conscious of their worth and keen to show their capabilities.

The only additional point I would make is that we may stop earning, but we never stop learning! Provided we follow the advice contained in this much-needed and well-written publication, we never will.

Sir Adrian Cadbury

Chancellor, Aston University

About this book

Career Skills: Opening Doors into the Job Market is a ground-breaking interactive aid for all students leaving an academic environment and moving into or returning to the world of employment. It is created from an employer's standpoint based on the extensive experiences of both human resource and line managers.

It is a personal 'tool kit' that . . .

- builds into a record of 'where I am today';
- provides a base to measure personal improvements for tomorrow;
- helps build confidence and self-assurance;
- removes fear and barriers at interview;
- introduces relaxation techniques to ease interview nerves;
- looks at the reasons behind different questioning techniques;
- explains business attitudes and needs;
- develops the individual's database;
- completes the 'ready to work' education process;
- starts developing networking skills;
- introduces communication skills – body language, listening, etc.;
- produces better prepared candidates for interview;
- provides structure to the 'get a job' project;
- advises on the attitude changes to be faced in organizations;
- provides a new 'life skill' within the world of work.

The 'tool kit' design provides ready-to-use material for each stage of the process. It features:

- step-by-step design;
- workbook format;
- a logical sequential approach;
- detailed guidance for CV production and letter writing;
- forms and control sheets to photocopy;
- model interview questions with guidance on answers;
- explanations of what recruiters look for;
- briefing of interviewers' techniques.

The workbook format gives career tutors training materials and classroom discussion topics.

The book is equally relevant to all school, college and university leavers. It:

● assists career counselling;
● provides self-assessment opportunities;
● focuses on personal achievements;
● complements the 'work experience' initiative;
● prepares students for university interviews;
● gives resources for mock interviews;
● forms the basis for curriculum development.

Career Skills: Opening Doors into the Job Market draws together the key elements of the job-search process into a single personal workbook using a step-by-step approach. The readers are given an insight into both the world of the recruiter and the process to follow to successfully pursue their chosen career path – whether in academia, public service or commerce.

All forms and control sheets are also available for downloading from the companion website: www.careerskills.org.uk.

About the writers

David Littleford

Prior to becoming senior partner in a specialist personnel consultancy practice he was the Group Human Resource Director of the UK subsidiary of the world's largest manufacturer and service provider of lifts and escalators. He also has extensive experience at both operational and senior executive level within the HR function of a major player in the UK motor industry. He has over 30 years' practical experience of the interactions between people and business with a special aptitude for coaching, counselling and mentoring young people entering the world of employment. He acts as a consultant to a number of exciting niche-market ventures in the UK and Europe, which include the development of management best-practice guides.

John Halstead

After qualifying as a professional accountant he has held a number of senior positions within both the finance and general management operations of various key service industries for over 30 years. During this period he gained extensive experience of people management and personnel techniques, and developed a special interest in promoting mentoring programmes for newly recruited graduates. This specialist interest, together with the experience of supporting and encouraging his own three children through their early career decisions, prompted him to join forces with David Littleford in the development of this project and various management best-practice guides.

Charles Mulraine

He has been responsible for communications strategy, planning and operations in three multinational corporations in 'f.m.c.g.' (fast moving consumer goods), manufacturing and engineering, and has worked in the USA, Europe and the Far East. For many years he managed his own consultancy and one of his current interests is as communications advisor to the International Partnership Network, which promotes the exchange of information and experience between education and business in countries throughout the world.

Preface

We passionately believe that individuals, when leaving full-time education, should be better prepared to secure employment in their chosen field and to continue their personal development. This view supports those of educationalists and employers who continually look to improve the effectiveness of the transition of individuals moving from the academic world into employment.

The challenge for students is to bridge the gap between the academic environment, and the commercial realities of working life. The size of the problem depends on the extent that the individual has been prepared for the change.

Whilst educationalists and employers work hard to bridge the gap, many people are still faced with a major obstacle to overcome when they leave full-time education, at whatever level. Work experience and project-based schemes help individuals to experience the working environment but do not tackle the fundamental task of 'getting a job' after qualification. From this basic need grew the concept of a 'tool kit' – effectively a series of Steps that include techniques, disciplines, formats and guidance notes gathered together in a workbook format, designed to be used by an individual at each stage of the process.

There are many good publications on various aspects of job-search preparation, be it in CV and letter writing, researching companies, aspects of the interview, etc. However, the uniqueness of *Career Skills: Opening Doors into the Job Market* is that it provides a totally different viewpoint on the process – we have collated our experiences as employers and passed them on to applicants. We have documented the skills and processes needed by applicants to plan and prepare themselves, obtain interviews and confidently face recruiters – with prior knowledge of the selection procedures and techniques used.

This personal workbook directs the reader through a logical sequence of steps to achieve the end result. It has been written by professionals in the fields of recruitment, motivation and communication . . . enabling students to see themselves through the eyes of recruiters.

We would like to thank the following for their contributions:
Christopher J. Lea, Ann Mulraine, Dr George Sik, Jacquie Worrall and Frances Wright.

David Littleford   **John Halstead**   **Charles Mulraine**

Introduction

The quality of a person's life is in direct proportion to their commitment to excellence, regardless of their chosen field of endeavour.

Vince Lombardi (1913–70), US football coach

You have purchased this workbook because you are looking to capitalize on your educational achievements to date as you start on your chosen career path. You may feel excited, nervous, eager, apprehensive, confident, concerned or any other emotion you can think of. You may have already tried the job market without success, or maybe you are just starting to look for that first 'career job'. You have spent the majority of your life so far in a series of structured academic environments with pre-determined goals and levels of reward dependent on your performance – relatively safe havens. Your only competitor was yourself, competing against the standards laid down, and not against your fellow students.

But now the 'world of work' is beckoning, the safety net has been removed and the competition really begins – *you* against everyone else looking for work.

The workbook has been designed for your personal use. It explains each stage of the job-search process and gives you support by providing practical and informed advice relevant to each particular task. The information and guidance we provide, combined with some determined hard work on your part, make anything possible. There is no substitute for good preparation and, when the interviews come along, you will have given yourself the best possible chance of success.

Our belief in the success of the process that we are advocating, when combined with your personal commitment, stems from extensive experience gained in working lifetimes of involvement in the recruitment world. This experience covered all aspects of the job market, from every standpoint – as applicants, recruiters and managers. We have seen what works and what doesn't work, what techniques fail and those that succeed.

Once you have fine-tuned the process to meet your personal needs, its value will increase. The skills and techniques you will learn form the basis of a repeatable 'life skill' that you can call upon as you develop your career.

How can I get a job – there are so few around and so many people going after them?

As we have said, our aim is to give you as much help, support and practical guidance as possible. We want to share our experiences with you in the hope that they will be useful, interesting and thought provoking. We are not here to make career choices for you – *you* have to make them, possibly with help from parents, friends, teachers, tutors and mentors. However, we do believe that we can help you to give yourself the best chance of achieving that first step on the career ladder – the critical first job.

Our experience has been gained over many years as employers and recruiters of high-calibre personnel. All too often we have been disappointed by the lack of preparation and research by candidates who have failed to sell themselves to us as worthwhile investments for the future. Their failure has been a direct result of their lack of understanding of the employer's expectations and needs.

There is always competition amongst employers for talented personnel. Candidates who sell themselves effectively and prepare well put themselves in the driving seat.

We are sharing our knowledge with you. We will tell you what to expect, how to handle problems and how to present yourself in the best possible light.

Choosing the career that will give you sufficient opportunities to channel your enthusiasm, interest and creativity for the next phase of your adult life – and generate financial reward – has become your new priority.

You may already have had lots of advice on career selection, researched the different routes, looked at all the alternatives available, discussed your ideas with parents, friends, etc., and made your choice on where you want to go and what you want to do.

If not, there is no time like the present to make a start. Whilst we can help you along the way to achieving your goal, it would be a good idea if you had a reasonable idea of what you want. Take advantage of all the careers advisory services available – they are there to help you.

The internet is an increasingly valuable information source for identifying career paths and opportunities. Some of the more progressive universities, government (DfES) and local authorities have developed excellent websites for this purpose. They are being added to regularly, and most can be easily accessed. Use one of the better search engines to identify them (www.google.co.uk; www.yahoo.com; www.msn.co.uk; www.ask.co.uk; etc.).

We have prepared a schedule (see Figure 1 below) for you to record your preferred websites for ease of future access. A copy of the form, to photo-copy, is provided in Appendix 4. A good starting point is www.connexions.gov.uk – well worth a visit.

Websites – career choices/job search*

* delete as appropriate.

List website addresses you have found which give access to good career choice information or assist with your job search (as appropriate)	Note information gained, for future reference – detail careers researched, etc. Cross-reference job searches with the job search campaign – control sheet'.

Figure 1   Websites – career choices/job search

I think, therefore I am

Descartes (1596–1650)

Step by step

Each Step of the workbook takes you through a separate stage of the process, and collectively they build a comprehensive guide to getting a job. How you use the workbook is up to you, but we suggest that you first read it through and select the key areas you may wish to concentrate on. However, don't forget that the stages are consecutive and therefore link with one another.

Step 1   Getting started looks at the early stages, at the ways you can plan your job search as if it were a marketing campaign or research project.

Step 2   Your personal sales 'tool kit' helps you to carry out your personal 'self-audit', discusses CVs and letters of application, and explains their importance to the recruiter. Issues of style, content and presentation are also covered.

Step 3   Searching for opportunities looks at the different ways in which information on careers, industries and employers can be found, and looks at the 'admin' you will need to do to keep track of your job search as letters go out and replies come in.

Step 4   Your interview 'tool kit' gives you guidance in preparing yourself for the interview, including your all-important response to the 'tell me about yourself' question, and examines the work you need to do just before the interview – including practising your presentations and reviewing your answers to possible questions.

Step 5   Communication tools is linked very closely to the previous Step and goes into this vital area in more depth, explaining how to understand and appreciate the effect communication has on others.

Step 6   The interview goes into interview protocol, types of interview and interviewer, and a few 'Do's and Don'ts'. The aim is to take the fear out of the unknown.

Step 7   After the interview looks at how to handle offers and rejections, and how to choose the best offer and agree terms.

Step 8   Into the future . . . gives you a quick look at what happens next as your career starts in earnest.

Appendices

Appendix 1 Style notes
Appendix 2 Sample curriculum vitae layouts
Appendix 3 Sample letters of application
Appendix 4 Forms for photocopying

College or university applications
Whilst the workbook is intended for use in the transition from academia to employment, the guidance offered can equally be applied to applications for college or university. Reading the workbook will help students appreciate the techniques that can be used in making applications, letter writing, and preparing for and handling interviews.

The people who get on in this world are the people who get up and look for the circumstances they want, and if they cannot find them, make them.

George Bernard Shaw (1856–1950)

Step 1

Getting started

Education is our passport to the future, for tomorrow belongs to the people who prepare for it today.

Malcolm X (1926–65)

This workbook has been prepared to give help, support, guidance and focus on the many and varied ways of entering the world of 'gainful employment'.

The workbook is not designed to make career choices for you. This is a highly personal decision and one that could be made in conjunction with one or more of the career advisory facilities that are available to you – see Step 3, 'Searching for Opportunities'. The timing of career choice is also up to you. Some organizations would suggest that taking advice before entering college or university will help you select the right establishment to best match your career aspirations. The workbook is intended to help with the process of carrying out the necessary research and to assist you in preparing yourself for the job selection process.

There is no instant formula for creating a successful career. So how do you start? Like most things in life there is no substitute for building on a solid foundation, and to help you focus your thoughts, the following principles will help you to establish your base line:

- Know what you want, and have a clear idea of your goals.
- Keep your senses active and be aware of your progress at all times.
- Finally, be prepared to adjust . . . until you get what you want.

You may change your mind, or adjust your goals. This should not be seen as failure or indecision, but rather as the product of an experience that has been learnt.

 It is not a mistake to turn back if you are on the wrong road.

Most of these principles are embedded in techniques for positive thinking and self-empowerment through the use of language and behavioural changes. One such technique is neuro-linguistic programming (NLP), which provides individuals with the 'know-how' to influence their own worlds. Dreams and reality can be very different, but when they combine, the result could turn 'just a job' into a rewarding and satisfying career. Further information is readily available on the internet – search for NLP or Richard Bandler (co-developer of NLP).

So do you know what you want to do?

Some of you will already have made your career choice. That's great. However, for anyone who is not totally convinced we suggest that now is a really good time to do a check on your thoughts, reasons and motivations.

> If you don't know where you are going, how can anyone else know? And that really is an interviewer's 'turn-off'.

If you are uncertain, then seek advice from trained careers counsellors at your school, college, university, etc., or do your own research into career opportunities that appeal to you.

Uncertainty and/or lack of enthusiasm will obviously have an impact on your motivation in the job search, and will ultimately show up to an experienced interviewer. *You* need to decide what *you* want – because without total commitment you will fail to realize your goals. You cannot influence potential employers if you are unclear in your thoughts of what you want to achieve.

So check your choice by asking yourself 'Do I really want to do it? Are my reasons for wanting this career path totally valid – or are they a whim (a dream without reality)?' The decision is yours. If *you* feel the decision is right, then go for it.

Procrastination is the thief of time.

Edward Young (1683–1765)

Where do I start?

A useful approach is to treat your job search as if it were a marketing campaign or research project. Campaigns of this type will normally be based on well developed plans covering market research, identification of customers, product design, promotion and sales effort.

Translated in terms of your job search:

- **market research**: identifies career opportunities in your chosen field;
- **customers**: are potential employers you may want to approach;
- **product**: is 'you' and the skills which have been developed that may satisfy the needs of your customers (potential employers);
- **promotion**: is the style and content of your sales material (that is your letters, CVs, telephone manner, etc.);
- **sales effort**: is the energy that you put into the whole process of getting the job.

Remember that you are trying to sell yourself by promoting your skills, enthusiasm and effort to an employer. The employers are looking to purchase your abilities in order to add value to their business or organization.

Market research

There are many sources of information to access.

- trade associations;
- websites;
- employment agencies;
- job centres;
- libraries;
- targeted companies;
- employer 'road show' visits;
- professional institutions;
- educational careers offices;
- career advisory services;
- trade magazines and periodicals;
- newspapers – national and local;
- career fairs;
- your network of contacts.

The internet offers the most accessible and immediate response. Sensible use of search engines will produce a wide range of priceless company information. This data can also help you identify companies you may wish to work for, and if so will provide valuable information when you are applying for employment.

Your network of contacts is an area of research that often has surprising untapped potential. A network is simply a list of all the people you know well enough to ask them for advice on where to pursue your ambitions and who you might approach in your job search. Your network may at first seem very limited, but once you begin to list your current and past contacts you will be amazed by the number of people that may offer help.

> Don't forget that when you ask your network contacts for help, you should ensure that you give them feedback on your progress and success.
>
> Politeness and courtesy cost you nothing and will enable you to visit the network again.

This isn't a one-off exercise, and your network will continue to grow with you. You in turn will be on someone else's network, and in the future you also will be called upon to assist others. Guard your network well and treat it with respect – people will respond positively to genuine approaches for help and guidance, but be careful not to take liberties.

Your market research will give you an abundance of information. All information is valuable and you need to be able to retrieve it quickly at any stage during your campaign. Keep good records. A good record system enables you to:

- rank the opportunities in order of preference;
- keep track of all the leads you are pursuing;
- update your network of contacts; and
- avoid the risk of embarrassment (and perceived incompetence) as a result of going to the same contact/organization twice asking the same questions.

We have included sample forms in Step 3 (see Figures 6 and 7) to help you in devising a simple tracking system. Copies of the forms to photocopy are provided in Appendix A.

Customers

You already have a reasonable idea of the career path you want to follow. Your research will have identified potential employers and now you should collect as much data as you can on each company/organization.

What information is needed? Basically, at this stage, anything that gives you a clear idea of where the business/organization has come from, where it is going, how successful it is and what its policies and aims are. Sources of specific information include:

- the website of the company/organization;
- local newspaper business pages for comments (most also have websites);
- recruitment advertising (developing companies/organizations need people);

- published marketing material, financial information, annual reports and brochures (ring the company/organization and ask what is available);
- libraries – research using trade directories, etc.

The concepts are simple but if you assess the data available in these sources you should be able to get a clear impression of each business/organization and whether it can offer the environment in which you would like to start/develop your working career.

The product, promotion and sales effort

A good deal of the remainder of this workbook is devoted to helping you prepare yourself for entry into the 'world of employment'. Our aim is to provide you with a 'tool kit' designed to give you the best chance of success in the job market.

The tool kit embraces 'product, promotion and sales effort' and should, for example, help you in the transition from the academic environment into the commercial world, with its completely new set of disciplines, standards of behaviour, work ethics and attitudes, which you will need to handle – if you want to succeed. The kit helps you to develop your personal promotional material (application letters and Curriculum Vitae) and your presentation at interview to achieve maximum positive impact.

> *All good things come to those who wait . . . but only what's left behind by those who seize their opportunities.*
>
> Abraham Lincoln (1809–65)

Step 2

Your personal sales 'tool kit'

> *The rung of the ladder was never meant to rest upon, but only to hold your foot long enough to enable you to put the other somewhat higher.*

> T. H. Huxley (1825–95)

Now you have a clear idea of what you want to do, it's time to get yourself ready for action. Leaving an academic environment, be it school, college or university, is an exciting prospect, but entering the world of work can be daunting, especially for those that have had no real work experience.

In the previous Step you decided what you wanted and started the process of preparing for the actions you need to take to achieve your goal; the next step is to prepare your promotional material to support your sales pitch.

Presenting the real 'me' – the product

Following the tactic suggested in the previous Step, that is to treat the job search as a marketing campaign, the next Step is to consider ways you can develop your promotional material and selling techniques.

Catalogue your experiences to date

In order to develop your CV effectively you need to catalogue all of those experiences in your life so far that could help you in your job application. At this stage you will not know which ones are valuable so you need to catalogue them all.

We have included an Experiences catalogue form (see Figure 2) for you to use. A copy of the form to photocopy is provided in Appendix 4. When you have completed your initial list, pick out all formative, significant or notable events. Then mark against each item the benefit, lesson, skill or special experience that resulted from it. Cover everything that has had some impact on you (whether positive or not) – the items could be drawn from experiences at school, college or university, or during your vacation or leisure time – list everything that you can recall. For example:

- vacation jobs at a supermarket – perhaps you helped introduce new staff, which developed your training skills;
- taking part in drama competitions may have developed public-speaking skills;
- voluntary work in a home for the disabled could have developed a whole range of life skills including working in a team.

Experiences catalogue form

Events or experiences	Analysis of the experience
List all the events that have occurred in your life so far – from school, college, university, home life, leisure or working time. Then highlight those that you feel are noteworthy.	For each highlighted experience, answer the question: 'What have I gained from that event or experience; how has it helped me develop as a person, or what lessons have I learnt?'

Figure 2   Experiences catalogue form

Strengths and skills 'self-audit'

In order to present yourself in the best possible light you need to have a clear understanding of your personal strengths, skills and areas that need developing. Why is this important? Your objective is to achieve employment in your chosen career and therefore you need to sell yourself. The purpose of this exercise is to help you develop a product that is attractive to an employer.

The next stage is to carry out a 'self-audit' to review and understand where your strengths, abilities, knowledge and skills actually lie – and to recognize any area that still needs to be developed. This isn't easy because natural modesty leads to a tendency to undersell, undervalue or not even recognize your strengths. Similarly it is easy simply to make excuses for areas that you feel less confident about – rather than being realistic and objective about them. The information on your Experiences catalogue form should prove to be helpful.

You might find it helpful to ask someone who knows you well to help with this exercise. Explain to them what it is you are trying to achieve and ask them to be honest and forthright – be ready for criticism and use it to clarify your thoughts. Friends will often highlight qualities that you had overlooked or undervalued.

Take the following steps using the Self-audit form (see Figure 3). A copy of the form to photocopy is provided in Appendix 4.

● Give yourself about five minutes to write down everything that comes into your head in answer to the questions 'What are my strengths? What am I good at?'
● Don't be modest – be proud of what you know and have achieved.
● Don't try to prioritize (but do be honest) – simply write down every-thing you can think of.
● Then repeat the process for 'What are my areas for development? What do I need to work at to improve?'
● Don't be too hard on yourself – these may be areas where you have had little experience to date.
● When you have finished you will have a lot of information and may need to clarify your notes to make them understandable at a future time.

The exercise highlights what you already know about yourself but puts it into a structured format. The information becomes valuable at various stages of the process:

● in preparing your curriculum vitae (CV) so that you can express your strengths clearly and concisely;
● helping to avoid over-exaggeration, which ultimately cannot be justified at interview;
● identifying your shortcomings prior to interview, which enables you to tackle them head-on and, if discussed at interview, to articulate your plans for improvement.

Try to review the results impartially. Be positive and enthusiastic about your achievements and experiences – be realistic about those areas that you feel

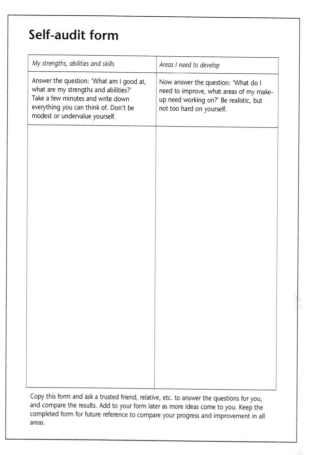

Self-audit form

My strengths, abilities and skills	Areas I need to develop
Answer the question: 'What am I good at, what are my strengths and abilities?' Take a few minutes and write down everything you can think of. Don't be modest or undervalue yourself.	Now answer the question: 'What do I need to improve, what areas of my make-up need working on?' Be realistic, but not too hard on yourself.

Copy this form and ask a trusted friend, relative, etc. to answer the questions for you, and compare the results. Add to your form later as more ideas come to you. Keep the completed form for future reference to compare your progress and improvement in all areas.

Figure 3   Self-audit form

are not your strengths, treating them objectively as areas that you are developing (and be ready to explain how you are doing it).

You already have qualities and capabilities that have been developed to a high degree. You know more about yourself than anyone else possibly can. No one knows what you really feel, think or fear. Your task is to sell your qualities in the best way possible while being, at the same time, realistic about the capabilities you will bring to any job you may be offered.

There is an issue of balance and reasonableness involved here. Overselling yourself could result in failure to meet an employer's expectations. This could lead to a loss of motivation and self-esteem, and ultimately to vulnerability within the job. Conversely, if you undersell yourself you put yourself at a risk of not getting the job you want in the first place, are likely to become frustrated, and ultimately could feel undervalued.

Remember that whatever you put in your material, an interviewer may use it as a source to interrogate your skills, competencies and motivation – 'what makes you tick'.

Your promotional material (CV and letter of application)

Why do I need a CV?

A curriculum vitae or 'CV', should be seen as quite simply your own personal selling advertisement. Like any sales advert it has to be suitable for your marketplace. There is no right or wrong way to write a CV, but some ways may be more effective than others. Content is crucial. Style can be more personal, and you should feel comfortable with the image your CV projects. You may be taking a risk if you decide to be totally unconventional in your presentation unless your marketplace warrants it.

The marketplace will initially judge you by your CV and letter of application. Their importance cannot be overstressed, in that:

● these two documents are, in effect, your passport to enter the world of employment;
● time invested in preparing the documentation to a high standard increases the likelihood of it being noticed;
● they help build self-confidence;
● the CV provides a solid base to develop your interview techniques;
● it provides the interviewer with a clear starting point that you feel comfortable with.

What do I put in my CV?

Recruitment specialists have differing views on the ideal length of a CV. Size may be relevant but not vital, especially at this early stage of your career. We suggest that no more than two pages is about right – but your view is equally valid. However, content is key and the CV must be factual, truthful, relevant and interesting.

Always put your name, address and contact details at the top of your CV to ensure that the recruiter can identify you easily. The remainder of your CV will record your personal details, education and qualifications, work experience and other relevant information, interests, hobbies etc. – but not necessarily in that sequence.

The requirement to 'present the real me' on a CV demands that you focus on your key strengths (these are your 'selling points'), and not on any less positive aspects of your make-up. This can seem to be a bit daunting, but if you tackle it in stages it becomes much simpler – use the CV working paper provided in Appendix A. There are six basic steps to follow – six sections in the CV.

Personal details

Personal details cover the basic information about you and should always appear at the start of your CV:

- name in full;
- address including post code;
- telephone and fax numbers;
- email address;
- driving licence and status (if appropriate);
- temporary contact points (if appropriate).

You may also decide to include your date of birth, marital status, dependants and health/disability status – these are not obligatory but employers may ask for the information at interview. This is an area where employers are cautious should the request for this information be construed as discriminatory.

Personal profile

A short, punchy, factual pen-picture of yourself and what you are about (briefly describing yourself to someone who doesn't know you). Omit the profile if you feel that it does not add value to your CV.

However, it is a good selling tool, a way of grabbing recruiters' attention and encouraging them to read on. The profile should be placed on the front page of your CV. This brief summary draws out the best factors about you and your make-up.

The profile should be well constructed and worded; if it is not there is a risk that it can act as a negative influence on the recruiter rather than a positive one.

Profiles should not normally exceed around 75 words and are usually made up of two or three elements:

- Your description of yourself, such as: *I am a highly motivated, confident and enthusiastic graduate with an aptitude for written and verbal communication.*
- Words describing what you are looking for and why, such as: *I have excellent computer skills and am looking for a stimulating and challenging position that will give me the opportunity to make a real and meaningful contribution.*

● If appropriate, you can also introduce between the other elements, some words describing where you are today, such as: *Since graduating I have acquired a basic grounding in business management techniques within the media distribution industry.*

The end product of the examples shown above would be:

I am a highly motivated, confident and enthusiastic graduate with an aptitude for written and verbal communication. Since graduating I have acquired a basic grounding in business management techniques within the media distribution industry. I have excellent computer skills and am looking for a stimulating and challenging position that will give me the opportunity to make a real and meaningful contribution.

Avoid repeating words within your profile. Usually repeats can be avoided by restructuring the phrases involved. For example, in the profile shown above, the first sentence was initially worded as: *. . . and enthusiastic graduate with excellent written and verbal communication skills.* The reworded sentence avoids repeating the words 'excellent' and 'skills' without any loss of emphasis.

The use of emotive words creates an image in the mind of the reader. Therefore, choose your words wisely and understand both what they mean and the impact they can have.

Refer to the list of 'key words' shown in the following section dealing with 'key skills'.

Key skills and achievements

Key skills include the abilities and competencies that you have developed to date and which can be transferred into the work environment. These could include organizational ability, administrative experience, leadership, decision making, communication skills (written and verbal), computer literacy, etc. Any achievements can be linked with the appropriate skill to give added emphasis.

Competencies are people's underlying individual characteristics, and may distinguish them from others. Competencies can be deep seated values, attitudes or beliefs, such as self-motivation or work ethic. They are not the specific tasks of a job; rather they reflect the individual's ability to carry out tasks effectively.

An effective way of highlighting the skills/achievements, and how they have been applied, is to use 'bulleted lists' constructed concisely and succinctly. Aim to use single sentences or phrases such as:

- strong communicator – represented university in national debating competition;
- good organizer – secretary of student archaeological society;
- highly competent in use of Excel, Word and PowerPoint, basic knowledge of Access.

Key skills should be placed strategically within the CV to catch the recruiter's eye as an important part of your 'sales pitch'.

The following lists give selections of strong words that may be useful as you build up your CV, and especially as you prepare both your 'key skills' and your profile.

Key words that describe you positively: 'I am . . .'

self-disciplined	self-reliant	self-confident	conscientious
diplomatic	discreet	tactful	persuasive
considerate	self-sufficient	ambitious	keen
motivated	enthusiastic	meticulous	painstaking
thorough	prudent	self-assured	positive
credible	perceptive	skilled	rational
independent	enquiring	careful	judicious
professional	coherent	excellent	flexible
logical	imaginative	creative	focused

Key words indicating motivational skills: 'I can/I am/I have . . .'

add value	administered	authorized	supervise
leadership	co-ordinated	make decisions	persuasive
ability	successful	developed	initiative
controlled	directed	managed	judgement
a winner	in charge	level headed	analytical
discerning	innovative	resourceful	inspirational
talent	aptitude	energy	drive

Key words to describe your competencies: 'I am/I have . . .'

creative	strength	ability	thorough
mastered	proficient	effective	talent
capacity	skilled	vigourous	competence
comprehensive	adept	strength	capable
aptitude	proficiency	expertise	faculty
lateral thought	initiative	discerning	innovative
enthusiastic	highly . . .	excellent	integrity

Educational records

Cover the academic establishments you have attended giving their names, dates attended, and the achievements and qualifications gained there:

- school (secondary onwards);
- college;
- university;
- colleges of further education;
- examinations, related grades and qualifications (be prepared to show certificates confirming your stated achievements);
- professional and vocational qualifications;
- current studies.

Avoid abbreviations other than generally accepted ones such as GCSE, BA, etc. If you have produced good work, a project, dissertation, thesis, etc., mention it but don't go over the top . . . just far enough to keep your customer's interest.

Employment experience – voluntary and vacational work

Work experience is unlikely to be extensive at this stage of your life, so make the most of the experience you have gained so far. Recruiters are looking for signs of your initiative, willingness to accept responsibility, and awareness of social needs, and indications of the type of person you are. For example, have you done any work involving supervision of staff, handling cash, etc?

Details of voluntary and vacational work that you have returned to on a regular basis can be grouped together, covering the overall period. It is worthwhile highlighting those activities that you may have been involved in, including those on a social or voluntary basis, where you have taken active responsibility.

Include any special skills that you have developed. Some of these may be relevant to the job you are seeking and others may have an interest value to the recruiter, who is looking at both abilities and personal achievements.

An obvious example of a work-related skill is computer literacy – you may be asked to demonstrate the level of ability you have in this area.

Whatever you have done in your spare/leisure time is worthy of note. You are your advertisement so don't hide your achievements, be proud of them and use them – others may be impressed. Brief details of your achievements can be noted under this heading or under the heading of 'Other interests' – the decision is yours. However, if you have a strong commitment to social or vocational work then it is best covered in this section.

Other interests

You should include hobbies and other interests, especially if they involve social and community activities. These activities are important – cover membership of societies, sports clubs/teams, etc. Detail any offices held at school, college or university. All these activities and the extent of your involvement give the recruiter clues about the real you and your interests. You should also include your achievements in any of the activities.

Constructing your CV

In the construction of your CV (and subsequent letter of application) it is important to use language efficiently. As the time available to a recruiter for reading is limited we have suggest that your CV should be contained within no more than two sides of A4 paper. Consequently it is vital that the written communication is succinct, unambiguous, clearly understandable and well constructed. Choosing the right and most appropriate words is a skill in itself. The construction of sentences and phrases will influence the reader. You must draw from tuition you have received within the academic world to meet this challenge – to put what you have learnt into practice for your own benefit.

When you have completed your initial draft, leave it for a couple of days and then go back and review it against your CV Working Paper. When you are comfortable with the draft you could try the following additional review techniques:

- Read it *out loud*, and listen to what you are saying (you could record yourself).
- Read the document to a friend (hearing the words, and not just reading them, helps you to recognize where words don't flow).
- Allow the friend to read the document.
- Ask your friend for feedback – if their understanding mirrors your intention you have succeeded.
- Ask your Careers Advisor to check your CV.
- As a final check ask someone to read your CV out loud to you.

> Too often we see what we want rather than what is actually written – so watch out for careless mistakes (for example, 'I am a perfectionist and rarely if if ever make mistakes').

If you like what you hear then move on – if not, re-write until you do like it and you feel comfortable with the CV and its contents. This advice applies equally to all correspondence associated with your job applications and follow-up letters.

What should my CV look like?
- Your CV represents you on paper.

- It must paint a picture of you which attracts the reader and encourages him or her to select it from the pile (without seeing or hearing you).

Having already prepared the 'goods' to go into the 'package', what will add value cosmetically and attract the curiosity of the reader?

There are a variety of innovative ways to design and structure your CV, but the basic appeal to the reader will stem from it being:

- logically sequenced for easy reading;
- consistent in style;
- uncluttered, straightforward with a fresh and crisp look.

Your CV will reflect your career, educational record, achievements, personal details and work/vocational experience in adequate detail. Avoid unnecessary padding or waffle. As your work experience may be limited it is unlikely that your CV will exceed two pages and in some cases it may only need a single page.

Ideally, use a word processor, but if you don't have one available you can, of course, and as a last resort only, handwrite your CV (and make sure any photocopies you take are of the highest standard you can get). Handwriting should be neat and legible. Print if you are one of Nature's little scribblers, but avoid alterations, smudges and the use of corrective fluids, even though it may mean a re-write.

Over-design, clip art, elaborate borders, brightly coloured and pre-printed paper can switch recruiters off (unless, for example, your goal is to become a graphic designer) – it is therefore a calculated gamble to embellish your CV in these ways.

CV design is very much a personal issue but remember that your CV presentation and contents should be designed to meet the needs of a prospective employer. The following are guidelines that can make a difference to your presentation.

- White space, that is blank space surrounding text, is helpful in giving an attractive presentation.
- Leave blank spaces and sensible margins – they give an impression of freshness and strong design.
- Use headings and indented paragraphs – they add interest and catch the eye.
- Use emboldened typeface or underlining to highlight important items, words or text – be careful not to overuse this technique and lose the impact.
- Avoid underlining CAPITAL letters.

- Use no more than two typefaces (fonts) on the page – for example, use Arial headings and Times New Roman for text.
- Construct sentences/phrases carefully and only use words you are familiar with and understand.
- Check spellings and grammar (don't always rely on the spell checker).
- Avoid waffle and don't try to be funny or cynical.
- Check for correct punctuation.
- Avoid using exclamation marks (!) to emphasize a point – your words should be sufficient.
- Make your comments clear and concise.
- Use good quality paper and envelopes (at least 80/90g).

It is your CV; it represents you so make sure that you feel comfortable with it. At all times keep in mind that the interviewer's role is to look beyond the packaging, and to 'feel the quality' of the product itself. Having attracted the attention of the recruiter, make sure that your CV speaks out and asks for an interview.

Varying your CV

Your CV should, in general, serve for the majority of job opportunities with little or no alteration. However, when you have identified the job you want and feel that you satisfy the requirements called for, you may decide to fine-tune your CV to match your specific skills or knowledge to the job. The match can be identified in your personal profile or in the main body of the CV.

This matching process can also be done in the letter of application, which you may find easier than continuously altering the CV. For example, 'I would like to draw your attention to my experience in . . .'.

Outlines of CVs showing layouts, etc., are given in Appendix 2, and see also Figure 4.

Overall layout is a personal issue, but in summary we would recommend that the following order of content is a good starting point:

- contact details (name, address, telephone numbers, etc.);
- personal profile;
- education details;
- key skills;
- employment experience;
- other interests, and the remainder of your personal details not shown at the front of the CV;
- referees (optional – names, status and contact numbers). Make sure you check *in advance* that the referees agree to support you.

CURRICULUM VITAE

Name:	Roger Peter SMITHSON
Address:	10 Goodby Avenue
	Upton
	Anytown
	AX4 2ZX
Telephone:	0111 222 3456
Email:	roger.smithson@people-perf.co.uk
Date of birth:	21 November 1981
Marital status:	Single

I am a highly motivated, confident and enthusiastic graduate with an aptitude for written and verbal communication. Since graduating I have acquired a basic grounding in business management techniques within the media distribution industry. I have excellent computer skills and am looking for a stimulating and challenging position that will give me the opportunity to make a real and meaningful contribution.

EDUCATION

| 1999-2003 | **University College Anytown** |
| | **BA (Hons) Business Studies and Law, Class 2.1** |

This specialised business course expanded my awareness of business management skills and law. The course covered the disciplines of sales, marketing, accounting and information technology, and involved a four-month work assignment with a marketing consultancy. My dissertation explored diversity within developing SMEs.

1997–1999	**St Leonards College, Anytown**	
	Sixth form college "A" Levels	1 – Grade A
		2 – Grade B
1992–1997	**De Montfort High School, Anytown**	
	GCSE	5 – Grade A
	GCSE	4 – Grade B
	GNVQ	2 – Distinction

I was awarded school colours in cricket, rugby, drama and swimming and captained the school cricket team.

KEY SKILLS

- Excellent verbal and written communication skills
- Strong interpersonal skills
- Computer literate – Word, Excel and PowerPoint
- Languages: French (fluent); German (conversational)
- Highly numerate
- Team player with proven leadership skills
- Full driving licence

Figure 4   Sample layout of CV

Headings and text fonts (typeface) to be consistent throughout. Never underline a heading typed in block capitals.

Work record since leaving college, university, etc. – if relevant. Show the important information briefly and highlight responsibilities, achievements, etc.

EMPLOYMENT

2004   **PNP Promotions**

Since graduating I was given a short-term contract to work with the Agency assisting with a project creating and delivering shareholder information for a major PLC.

VACATION JOBS

2002–2003   **PNP Promotions**

Promotions Assistant – This was a four-month placement and I gained experience of general promotional activities, advertising, administration and creative development work. I was subsequently given the chance to do vacation work with the Agency and the experience gained has been the major reason behind my choice to work in the media.

Vacation jobs should be grouped if repeated. Give appropriate detail. Include any voluntary or community work.

1999–2001   **Anytown Advertiser**

Reporter (vacation work) – This was my first experience of working in the media, and working as a trainee reporter taught me how to source and tailor stories to the specific target audience. It was also my first experience of working in a highly pressurised and time-sensitive environment. Three of my articles were published.

1998–1999   **Hornbeam House** (Anytown)

Volunteer – This work involved caring for mentally ill residents and the organisation of various therapeutic group activities. The residents were all young adults.

1997–1998   **Anytown Social Services**

Ambulance Guide – The role of this position included care work for severely mentally ill patients during transport to and from special care centres. I was also actively involved with patient care and the organisation of group activities at the centres.

PERSONAL INFORMATION

At University I was a member of the film-making club and wrote regularly for the in-house magazine. I enjoy film and drama, comedy, literature, music and most sports, playing at football at weekends. I also enjoy travelling (both this country and abroad) and experimenting with vegetarian cookery. I am passionate about environmental and conservation issues and do voluntary "hands-on" work for the Footpaths and Walkways Association.

Show any personal data not on first page. Include hobbies, interests, etc.

REFEREES

Mr David Davidson, Tutor, University College Anytown,
The High, Anytown AX1 1AA. Telephone: 0111 101 2321.

Mrs Jocelyn Jones, Director, PNP Promotions,
PNP House, Grange Drive, Anytown AX1 3ED. Telephone: 0111 199 5555.

Choose whether to show referees. If shown, at least one should be academic.

The final choice of style and content is personal and you should feel comfortable with the end product.

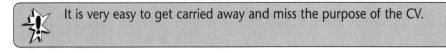

It is very easy to get carried away and miss the purpose of the CV.

Use of referees

Most employers will require you, at some stage of the process, to provide at least one, normally two, references from individuals who can provide quality information about you. Referees should be chosen with care and be well known to you and you to them. They will be expected to be able to comment on some or all of your academic ability, work application, character, social skills and interests, and to give an overall recommendation.

The standing or status of the referee within business, academia or society is important and can add value to your reference.

You must always make sure that your referees are prepared to provide references, before nominating them. Keep your referees up-to-date with the progress you are making and advise them of the outcome. They will appreciate this common courtesy.

Use your network of connections to identify the most appropriate referees.

Your letter of application

As previously stated, there are two pieces of information the recruiter needs during the initial 'trawl' through applications – the letter of application and the CV. Whilst the CV contains specific detail about you, the letter is your chance to introduce your CV, and to draw attention to your strengths, abilities and experiences which have specific relevance to the job opportunity you are applying for.

The letter is, therefore, vitally important as it carries the responsibility of the first impression. Realistically a poor first impression is as good as the kiss of death to your application, and if your letter does not catch the eye of the recruiter, your CV may not even be read.

So what are the ways of creating this 'letter appeal'? Remember your marketplace. You are trying to attract a positive reaction from the job market, so write your letter in a formal (not casual) way.

This means sensible styling, neatness, good grammar and spelling, concise and clear content with a beginning, a middle and an end. Above all, if you are responding to an advertisement, your letter should identify the source (that is the newspaper or periodical in which it appeared) and should highlight any relevant experience and achievements that match those asked for in the advertisement. If you are asked to 'apply in your own handwriting' you must do so. There is probably a very good reason for this instruction and a printed or typed letter will simply go straight into the 'reject' pile, together with those applications that are poorly presented.

The only exception to this rule is if you are unable to comply because of a disability. Under these circumstances you should make it clear why you have not followed the instruction.

Content

The content of your letter is vital to your application. A 'standard' or mediocre letter will not differentiate you from the 'crowd'. Every vacancy and its requirements is specific to the business/organization recruiting and will be different. Therefore, each letter has to be designed for the needs of the individual job opportunity. It should be clear and precise, targeted specifically to the opportunity, written in good clear language with no slang, abbreviations or obscure words, and above all it should read well.

Ideally the letter should be typed, or neatly written, on no more than one side of paper. It must have:

- your name and address;
- your contact telephone number;
- the name, job title, address of the person you are writing to (make sure it is complete *and* correct);
- the date;
- any reference codes shown in the job details or advertisement.

The body of the letter will usually have just three paragraphs:

- Paragraph 1 should explain why you are writing, giving details of the advertisement, etc., that you are responding to.
- Paragraph 2 should highlight, in a couple of sentences, your experience, skills, aptitudes and so on that are particularly relevant to the job as described in the advertisement, etc.
- Paragraph 3 completes the letter and will include your request for an interview.

The letter is a formal letter and should be written in short, confident phrases and sentences. Words should be strong, positive and confident (refer to the lists in the 'Key skills' section earlier in this Step). Avoid jargon,

Figure 5   Sample layout of letter of application

The annotations around the figure read:

- Date, in 'dd mm yyyy' format. Name, job title and address of person you are writing to – make sure it is correct.
- Your address – use printed stationery or (if word processed) use a different font or style, such as italic.
- Salutation – make sure you check the spelling.
- Allow three or four lines between the address and salutation.
- Title of the job, underlined or in bold type – show any reference number.
- Notice the spacing paragraphs.
- Paragraphs in this letter are 'blocked' – i.e. not indented.
- Position the letter carefully on the page. If a newspaper or magazine is referred to, show the title in inverted commas.
- Your name is underlined
- Leave about five lines for your signature.

The sample letter reads:

24 Goodby Road
Upton
Anytown
AX4 2QF
Telephone: 0111 222 4466
Email: rebecca.chamberly@people-perf.co.uk

30 June 2004

Mrs P H Stonehousen
General Manager
AnyCo Limited
200 Commercial Road
Anytown
AA1 7AS

Dear Mrs Stonehousen

Graduate Trainee Scheme

My research into your Company indicates that you may be recruiting graduates in the summer for full time positions. I was particularly interested in the product information on your web site and the statements you make about your ambitions and goals which I find attractive and exciting.

Rather than waiting for the graduate recruitment fairs and advertisements I am approaching you now as I believe that I have the educational background and qualities that you may be looking for. My degree course is Business Studies and Law and I am predicted to achieve a Class 2.1. I am enthusiastic by nature and thrive on responsibility and team-work. I am willing to learn and have excellent communication skills together with a good sense of humour.

I enclose my CV for your information and would welcome the chance to meet you and discuss possible opportunities.

Yours sincerely

Rebecca Chamberly (Ms)

abbreviations and words not in common usage. Appendix 1 gives more detailed suggestions on style and layout, and see Figure 5.

Try reading the letter out loud or to a close friend – the latter is probably the most effective way of checking for sense and 'readability'. Be ready for criticism and accept it as constructive. You may not agree with the comments (and decide not to change anything) but don't react by taking a defensive or argumentative attitude – don't lose a friendship or advisor over the issue.

If you take the trouble to personalize the letter the recruiter will recognize this and appreciate your efforts. If you simply mass-produce your letter it will look more like a circular than a serious application, and circulars quickly find their way to the bin.

Appendix 3 contains a series of template letters covering a range of situations.

An example of how a poorly constructed letter can be improved is shown below. By careful editing the letter displays better structure, uses fewer words, is easier to read and comprehend, and has eliminated the basic errors (that is, not addressing the letter to an individual and incorrect sign off).

BEFORE

Dear Sir/Madam

I am writing to Cosmo International to enquire about Graduate Trainees. I am a Business Studies Student at West Ridge University looking for a 12 month paid placement. I am available from July 2004 – September 2005. I have a keen interest in the media industry especially the marketing/PR side and have been taking an interest in Cosmo International since its launch. I want to work for a progressive, dynamic market leader with a strong brand reputation and feel that Cosmo International fulfils these criteria.

I am a committed, creative, reliable, enthusiastic and highly motivated individual with communication skills, thirst for knowledge and enjoy a challenge.

I have enclosed my CV. If you need any further information or would like me to attend an interview I would welcome the opportunity to do so.

Yours sincerely

Nathalie Dupont

AFTER

Dear Mr Simpson

Graduate Trainee opportunities with Cosmo International
As a Business Studies Student at West Ridge University, I am seeking an opportunity with your company for a 12-month paid placement between July 2004 and September 2005. Having an interest in the media industry, I first became aware of Cosmo International when it was launched in 2000. I am looking to join a progressive and dynamic market leader with a strong brand reputation to gain experience and make a contribution.

My interests are business in general but with a focus in marketing, customer care and product promotion. I have enclosed my CV high-lighting my skills and motivation.

I would welcome the opportunity to discuss this further.

Yours sincerely

Nathalie Dupont

Occasionally, recruiters restrict the number of words to be used in the letter of application – say to 100 words. These requirements must not be ignored. You can highlight your characteristics and strengths by referring to your CV rather than describing them in the letter.

Style (layout)

Your letter of application is a formal letter and it makes sense to lay it out in a professional way. Appendix 1 provides some suggested guidelines on both layout and style. These guidelines apply whether your letter is produced by word processor or handwritten. The former, however, obviously gives you greater flexibility to tailor the letter. The goal is to produce a letter which looks good and passes your message efficiently to the reader.

Applications by email

Special care should be taken with email applications. You have control over the quality of presentation of a written application, but with email, control is limited by the recipient's system. It is important to check that attachments are in a format that can be read by most computers – word processed documents or pdf files should be acceptable, but must be limited to a single attachment – multiple attachments have a high nuisance value. Don't be too informal in the manner of address – avoid being too casual or 'chatty'. Before you send an email, check the content, make sure you have attached the correct file – check twice; send once. Use your virus checker to ensure that the email is 'clean'.

What happens to your letter of application and CV?

To make an initial selection of potential candidates for the vacancy advertised, employers require information. This information usually comes in the form of the CV and letter of application. However, some employers require a company application form to be completed as well as, or in place of, a CV. If this is the case, and provided that you have prepared a good CV, it should present little difficulty in transferring the information from the CV to the application form.

If you are asked to complete an application form, complete it *fully* – don't fall into the trap of simply referring to your CV. However, always attach a copy of your CV to the application form, and refer to the fact in the covering letter, for example: '. . . I have also enclosed a copy of my CV for your information.'

Your application details may be amongst tens, even hundreds of applications for any vacancy.

The process

A recruiter will probably have a restricted amount of time available to filter the applications and will usually split the task into several stages.

Stage One is the initial 'trawl', where the applicant's letter is subject to the trained eye of the recruiter (for say 20 seconds) who is looking for relevance to the job and good presentation. If the letter passes this check the CV goes through a similar process culminating in an 'Accept/Reject' decision at this point. This may seem to be unfair but the decision is very subjective – with high volumes of applications there is often no viable alternative for the recruiter. Those rejected at this stage are normally held for a short time, as it is possible they may be revisited if the next stage does not produce sufficient potential candidates.

During the next step, Stage Two, the recruiter gives each letter and CV accepted at Stage One a much closer examination, and assesses each application against the needs of the job. The applications which closely match the job are submitted for interview; the remainder are usually held in reserve.

Hopefully, you will have realized by now just how vital the letter of application and CV are to opening that first door.

> Time to 'go to press' – are you happy with the way that 'You' look on paper?

'Every picture tells a story'

Proverb

Telephone job applications or enquiries

Effective use of the telephone is a serious communication technique that businesses/organizations rely on. In your job search you may have to make contact by telephone to obtain information or enquire about job prospects.

Whether or not you are comfortable with using the telephone there are a number of simple techniques and guidelines that you might find useful. These techniques are similar to those that you will use in an interview situation (covered later in the book). The obvious main difference is the lack of any visual contact. You will, of course, have all your other senses available to you.

Simple techniques to think about

- Imagine that you are face-to-face with the person you are calling, and act accordingly – that is, have a normal conversation and smile when you speak.
- The first person you speak to is most likely to be a receptionist – treat them with respect, as poor impressions travel fast within an organization.
- Be friendly and think positively; do not be offhand or superior at any time even if the person you are speaking to is curt or unfriendly.
- Have a notebook and pencil ready to take notes of what is being said – don't rely on your memory.
- Prepare yourself in advance – write down what you want to say.
- Know what questions you want to ask.
- Avoid 'waffle' – be clear in what you are going to say.
- Find a quiet place to make/take the call if possible (away from disruptions).
- Prepare for the unexpected – interruptions, disconnections, crossed lines and aggressive/protective secretaries.

It is not unusual to be nervous about using the telephone but good preparation helps. The best solution is to practise.

Get a trusted friend or member of your family to take part in 'role-play'. Whilst it is not the real thing, role-play can be made to be realistic and should help overcome your discomfort. You could practise by recording messages – then listen to the recording and review your technique until you feel comfortable with the result. For example, is your message clear, do you sound confident, did you gabble, did you waste valuable time by waffle or by being vague about the purpose of the call, were there too many 'uhms', 'arhs' or 'you knows'?

Remember that if you need to leave a message on an answer phone there may be a limited time for you to record your message, so use the time well. Always start your message by stating your name, and the time and date of your call, the job reference and your contact number.

Step 3

Searching for opportunities

Find out what you like doing best and get someone to pay you for doing it.

Katherine Whitehorn (born 1926)

Finding job opportunities requires focus, perseverance, energy and determination coupled with the ability to be alert, to listen and to investigate. Job opportunities are all around – the key is knowing where to search.

The most obvious areas to start looking for job opportunities are:

- advertisements in the media – newspapers, professional or special interest magazines, radio, television, etc.;
- careers teachers/advisors at your school, college or university;
- careers fairs and employer 'road show' visits;
- websites;
- employment agencies – general and specialist;
- government sponsored career advisory services, etc.;
- careers centres or job centres.

Less obvious, but equally effective, areas to search include:

- networking;
- cold calling;
- news items in the business/financial/academic media (newspapers, television, radio), where employers predict expansion, new products, etc.

Use all of these channels if appropriate to your needs. The more 'irons you have in the fire' the better.

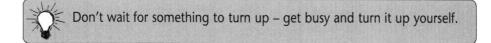 Don't wait for something to turn up – get busy and turn it up yourself.

Careers advisory services, careers fairs, etc.

Make full use of the opportunities available in your school, college or university. They are staffed by specialists whose objectives are to help you find the right job opportunities. Most schools, colleges and universities have established (locally, regionally or nationally) good communication links with potential employers. These links have developed over time:

- at school level, through work experience projects;
- at further education colleges and universities, where partnership schemes have been developed with employer organizations.

When you leave, keep these contacts alive as part of your networking activities.

Networking

What is networking?

A network is a simple, informal structure made up of a series of communication links between people. Businesses and organizations use networking as a major method of developing relationships – gaining information to promote the business/organization and its products or services.

Your network grows every time you meet someone new.

Networking, in this context, requires you to establish and list the links you have with people you know, and those with whom you have a common interest or association through work, friendship, pastime or other activities. When you make a contact, your network grows by that person. Remember that, as a result of this new contact, that individual's network also links into yours (similarly, you are added to theirs).

Imagine you have 10 key contacts and each of them has 10 key contacts, and each of them has a further 10 contacts – your network now has the potential of reaching 1,000.

Even though some of these contacts may appear in several of the networks, the potential power of this cascade effect is awesome – and with nurturing can be a very useful tool throughout your career.

When spiders unite they can tie down a lion

Ethiopian proverb

You may consider that your existing contacts are limited at the moment. However, if you examine the list of people you know, you already have the basis of a network. This will include friends, family, teachers, tutors, mentors and acquaintances and will provide a solid base for you to start from. These contacts have their own networks, which they may allow you to use. The extent of these linked networks of contacts can be surprising, and people are usually willing to help if they can – provided they are asked properly and don't feel that they are being imposed on.

 Guard your network well and treat it with respect – people will respond to genuine approaches for help (but **do not** take liberties).

It is worth taking time to look at networking techniques more closely. Developing, building and maintaining an effective network properly is a skill that needs effort. It can pay handsome dividends at any time, providing you:

● have the respect of the person whose support you are seeking;
● recognize that losing that respect will damage your reputation.

For networking to succeed there are a number of basic disciplines and requirements, including:

● creating a positive impression on people;
● ensuring your contacts have confidence that your motives are genuine;
● developing, maintaining and updating a system of recording and recalling the names and activities of your contacts;
● categorizing your contacts in order of importance – close friends, relatives and associates (the ones most likely to help); acquaintances; and finally, contacts referred to you by others;
● keeping in touch with your network (in particular, close friends and associates) – not just when you need something;
● informing the contacts used for help of the outcome and progress made;
● responding to your network in the way you would want the network to support you;
● listening and remaining alert – information on job opportunities can come from anyone;
● keeping your network record up-to-date as it grows.

Networking is actually an everyday habit we are involved in without thinking about it. The skilled networker organizes and structures the information gathered over a long period of time and calls upon it as a possible source of information, help or reference in, amongst other things, job seeking.

The way you record your network information is a matter of personal choice: for example, business cards, simple index cards, address books, electronic aids, etc. Store the information in a way that enables you to retrieve it quickly. The information you collect will build a database of invaluable contacts over time. A Networking control sheet is included in Figure 6. A copy of the form to photocopy is provided in Appendix 4.

Networking control sheet

Contact name	Telephone, fax, email details	Contact code*	Introduced by**	Details of approach/request	Outcome of approach	Follow up†

Note: * Contact codes 1. Known to you personally; 2. Met (introduced by a friend); 3. Not met (friend recommended approach).
** Details if not directly known to you.
† If the contact comes from a network contact remember to advise them of the outcome of the approach and thank them for their help.

Figure 6   Networking control sheet

Cold calling

Cold calling is another accepted selling practice, where people are approached, uninvited, to try to create sufficient interest in a product so that a sale can be made.

This method is also used in job searches; the only difference here is that *you* are the product.

Having decided on the career path that you want to follow, the next step is to identify the companies or organizations that could be approached.

Research will provide the contact names within each organization, details of locations, products, performance, etc. Ringing the organization and asking for the names of key staff (Personnel Manager, General Manager, etc.) is logical as it will ensure you have totally up-to-date information. Always make certain that you check the correct spelling of names, addresses, etc., and confirm job titles when gathering information.

Develop a script explaining your reasons for approaching the organization – for example:

'I am an engineering graduate and have read about the expansion of your product range in the business press. If possible I would like to come along to

discuss with you what opportunities you may have for graduates, now or in the future.'

You may also give further details about your qualifications and your special interests. If the initial response is negative, suggest that you will send your CV for their future consideration, and then after a period of, say, two weeks, follow up by confirming whether your papers have been received and checking if there has been any change in their recruitment situation.

Vary your approach by using telephone, email or letter – try all three methods. The telephone is the most direct and instantaneous, but see which approach most suits your style.

If you are particularly keen to join a specific organization or business you may consider offering to 'job shadow' to gain experience. Job shadowing is a practice where an organization permits an individual to follow closely one of their employees in the day-to-day work environment. This has three main advantages:

- gaining first-hand experience of the organization, the people, work and culture;
- becoming known to the employer and having the opportunity to impress;
- enhancing your CV with relevant experience and showing initiative.

The disadvantage is that you should expect that normally these positions are unpaid. However, some organizations make some form of payment to cover expenses.

Above all, don't get despondent. Cold calling is possibly the hardest of all the routes and as such your 'hit rate' (results achieved compared with approaches made) will be the lowest. However, you only want one job – so keep going.

If, as a result of a cold call, you are invited to 'pop in for a chat' make sure that you are well prepared. Treat the meeting as an interview – with the same principles of preparation, conduct and seriousness.

Advertisements

Look through recruitment advertisements in the press. Most national and regional papers have special days – check which they are, for example many of the 'quality' nationals run ads on Thursdays and Sundays. They also often run special features aimed at people leaving school, college or university.

The job advert sometimes provides the background to the company and the purpose of the role for which it is recruiting, but not always. It is advisable, therefore, to do some research into the background of the company before replying. This can tell you about the company's values, strategies, products and future developments, which may be useful to refer to in your application. It will certainly be of value should you be selected for an interview.

Use your tool kit as the basis for your replies to advertisements and remember to personalize each letter.

Websites

There is an increasing variety of specialist recruitment websites offering routes to job opportunities. A growing number of companies are recognizing the potential of the Internet to reach wider audiences, and use their own and online recruitment sites to advertise job opportunities. The advantages to employers are:

● the size of the potential market;
● speed – jobs are advertised quickly without the need to conform to newspaper press deadlines; and
● the fact that their opportunities will be included on a searchable database accessible by potential candidates.

Use your IT skills to search them out and see 'what is on offer'. Such sites often offer advice on job searching, so time spent exploring them can be very helpful. Every available opportunity warrants in-depth research.

Job search campaign – control sheet

Make a list of all the contacts and names that you have decided to approach – use a simple form to do this (have a look at the layout in Figure 7). Make sure you collect as much information as possible from your network database – names, job titles (titles can be very important to people in all organizations – give someone the wrong title and, believe it or not, you could blow your chances), telephone numbers, addresses, etc. Rank these prospects according to their appeal (be realistic *and* positive). Use it as your Action Control. A copy of the form to photocopy is provided in Appendix 4.

Making your approach and securing an interview

You have identified the business/organization you want to approach. The first step is to fine-tune the research you started earlier in order to

Job search campaign – control sheet

Organization name and address	Telephone, fax, email details	Contact name	Source	Vacancy	Dates of contact	Interview Yes/No	Comments/outcome

Note: If your source comes from your network, remember to advise your contact of the outcome of the approach and thank them for their introduction and help.

Figure 7   Job search campaign – control sheet

get maximum information. This will allow you to tailor your letter of application appropriately and incorporate comments that are relevant to that business/organization. The research also gives you information to use if you are called for interview – for example, knowledge of their products, philosophies, goals, social awareness, development programmes, history and financial performance.

Use the guidance given in Step 2 to develop your letter of application.

Once you have made your applications you have to wait a reasonable time for responses. It is not unusual for two or three weeks to elapse before you get a reply as most jobs have a large number of applicants. If a closing date has been advertised then you may receive an acknowledgement, but this is not guaranteed. Patience can be a virtue – it can also be seen as a lack of interest, therefore a follow up on your application after a sensible amount of time might be appropriate.

When you receive a positive response you have a short time before the interview in which you can complete your preparations (see Step 4) and any research you wish to make on the company/organization. You could consider making a 'spying visit' to the location, preferably during a working day, to get a feel for the environment, and to check transport arrangements and local amenities. You might discover where other employees go for lunch – relevant information can sometimes be overheard – and you can get a flavour of the local culture.

Step 4

Your interview 'tool kit'

Until you try you don't know what you can't do

Henry James

This section is designed to help you prepare for the day of the interview. Step 6 will show you how the interview may take shape and give you guidance on the stages involved in the process.

Remember, all face-to-face interviews will be different – we are all individuals and are completely unique. Whilst interview styles will vary, the underlying structure that most companies adopt is similar, and has:

- an introduction – welcoming and putting you at ease;
- a brief summary of the business/organization, its products, goals, etc. (some interviewers may test your knowledge about the business/organization, to see what research you have done);
- structured general and specific questions aimed at finding out about the 'real' you – your responses will generate follow-on questions;
- the closing – an opportunity for you to ask any final questions you may have, including seeking initial feedback; the interviewer may ask how you felt about the interview, and will usually provide details of the next stages in the process.

The face-to-face interview may form only part of the total interview process, which could involve role-play, group discussions and psychometric testing. These other aspects will be covered in more detail in Step 6.

Throughout interviews, patterns of behaviour will develop between you and the interviewer, normally initiated by an individual interviewer's style. Skilled interviewers attempt to obtain as much relevant information as possible in the limited time available and they will create an environment to achieve their objectives. You cannot predict an interviewer's style but you can pre-plan and decide how best you can make an impression. Always remember that you need to be in control of your own behaviour.

Don't forget that the interview starts the moment you walk into the room – before words have been exchanged. All of the following elements convey information about you to the interviewer, so you should consider each item and prepare yourself and practise where appropriate:

- **Dress code:** You don't need to wear a business suit but make sure your clothes are clean, smart and not too casual; ties, if appropriate, should not be loose; select clothes that are not too tight and that allow you to sit with decorum; make sure footwear is clean.
- **Hair:** Neat, tidy and clean – facial hair should be well groomed.
- **Jewellery:** Your decision, but be aware that many people can be biased against facial jewellery in particular.
- **Greeting:** Handshakes firm but *not* bone crushing; be genuine.
- **Manners:** Sit down only when invited; remember basic manners.
- **Body language:** Keep eye contact but don't stare; control hand movements and don't fidget.
- **Posture:** Walk tall, sit up and don't slouch.
- **Facial expressions:** Smile when appropriate and look interested.

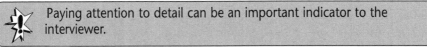

Paying attention to detail can be an important indicator to the interviewer.

Cultural awareness

Interviews will vary in approach and will be influenced by the culture within the employer's business, industry or organization. In this sense, 'culture' covers customs and practice – dress code, method of address (formal or informal), etc. However, cultural issues also involve national and regional characteristics, beliefs and traditional ways of life.

It is very important to research the potential employer's business/organization to identify its cultural conventions. Avoid being misled by stereotypical images and perceptions that have developed over the years through humour and the media. Examples include the laid back Australian, the careful Scotsman, the boring accountant, the casual American and the hard-hat brigade from the oil and construction industries. You will have experienced multi-cultural exchanges during your time at college or university. Again, avoid being misled by clichés – the British reserve, the Latin temperament, the Germanic formality and the African flamboyance.

There are always differences between cultures at whatever level – respect the differences and work with them.

To understand these differences you will have to take your lead from whatever contact you make with the employer, be that receptionist, secretary or interviewer. Learn to think on your feet and follow the leads given. It is hard to rectify mistakes after the event – words once spoken, are difficult to retract.

Step 5, 'Communication tools', helps you to prepare for the interview situation, where you will need to be sensitive to these issues.

> Prepare for aggressive interviewers by practising self-control – it costs nothing to be polite and can have big rewards.

Preparing for the questions

> *I keep six honest serving men (they taught me all I know): their names are What and Why and When and How and Where and Who.*
>
> Rudyard Kipling (1865–1936)

There are a number of standard or general questions that the interviewer may ask as 'ice breakers', on the basis that you will have a fairly clear idea about your answers. This will be intended to help you relax and settle your nerves.

Ice-breaker questions

Pleasantries:

- How did you get here?
- Did you have trouble finding us?
- Were the instructions OK?
- Did you get the details we sent?

Openers:

- Tell me a bit about yourself.
- What attracted you to our company/organization?

Keep your responses to these questions crisp and short. If the interviewer wants to know more, follow-on questions will be asked.

Detailed questions

The interviewer will quickly move on to the main agenda – the detailed questions that are intended to find out about you. Normally the interviewer will be well prepared with questions aimed at getting to know:

- you and your personality;
- your likes and dislikes;
- your qualifications;
- your achievements;
- your competencies and skills;
- whether you are a team player or prefer to work on your own;
- your work style and ethic.

The above groups of questions are designed to see if you fit the requirements of the job and the culture of the company/organization.

 Imagine going into an interview knowing that you will be faced with this pattern of in-depth questioning without being prepared.

Be prepared for the interviewer to put the questions in a different way. By understanding the purpose of the question you will be able to prepare answers that will adapt to the question.

 Relying on answers to the model questions will not be enough – make sure you prepare yourself fully.

Model questions

We have included work sheets listing an extensive selection of the type of questions that are likely to be asked at interview. These model questions are not intended to be definitive or exact. The purpose, therefore, is to get you used to the *type* of questions you can expect to face, and to help you prepare your own answers to these or similar questions, to put you in a position to be prepared to give considered replies.

The comments listed on the work sheet are offered as 'thought provokers'. You have to provide your own responses based on your own circumstances, opinions and preferences – but always try to construct your thoughts optimistically (a pint glass half full – *not* half empty). Note your thoughts in the space provided in the work sheet, for future reference.

However, don't memorize the questions or your answers, because like exam papers, the questions will not be asked in the way you expected.

We have grouped the questions into sections that identify the type of information the interviewer may be seeking. The question headings are as follows.

- introductory questions (1–4);
- questions related to the job opportunity (5–14);
- questions to identify your leadership style (15–21);
- questions about your academic experience (22–33);
- questions about you, your attitudes and achievements (34–45);
- questions about your experiences away from an academic environment (46–50);
- questions searching for specific competencies (51–5).

Use the continuation template (56–65) to record additional qustions you have been asked, or think may be asked.

Model question work sheet

Potential questions	Observations
Introductory questions	
1. How are you? Did you get here OK? Any difficulty with the traffic? etc.	*A gentle way to let you settle into the interview environment – be grateful.*
2. Tell me a little bit about yourself.	*This is a preliminary 'warmer' question to settle you into the interview. Make your response brief, cover your personal details, for example age, school, college, university, interests, hobbies, etc. (as detailed on your CV).*
3. What do you know about our company and what we do?	*This is where your research comes in – shows the interviewer how interested you are in the job and the company.*
4. How have you prepared for this interview?	*Explain what resources you drew on to research the company and job – this again shows the level of your interest.*

Questions related to the job opportunity	
5. How did you hear about the vacancy?	*Tell them – network, advert, personal contact, phone or written enquiry, etc.*

Notes for your response

'Sit upright and keep alert and listen'
1.
2.
3.
4.

'Be positive and smile'
5.

Potential questions	Observations
6. What do you think our main business objectives are?	*Look for their Vision or Mission Statements or comments in the accounts and their website, and be ready to build the principles into your answers.*
7. How will your academic achievements assist you in the post you have applied for?	*Explain that the disciplines of your academic experience in research, critical analysis and ability to absorb information are transferable skills into the world of business – irrespective of the actual qualifications achieved.*
8. What do you think you will contribute to the company?	*A chance to sell yourself and your special skills – don't undersell yourself.*
9. How does this job opportunity fit with your personal career plans?	*Explain how the job fits with your aims and goals.*
10. Have you any other interviews in the near future?	*Tell them – however, if you have other interviews it is your choice whether to disclose who they are with.*

© David Littleford et al. (2004), *Career Skills*, Palgrave Macmillan Ltd

Notes for your response

6.

7.

8.

9.

10.

Potential questions	Observations
11. What do you expect the company to provide?	*This is an opportunity to state what you are looking for in terms of career progression, development, job experience, and training to meet your expectations and aspirations. This is in addition to the general contractual terms of salary and benefits.*
12. What are your salary requirements?	*This depends on a number of factors – your needs, what you feel you are worth and how much you want the job. This might be your first experience in the art of negotiation. Have a salary range in your mind – some jobs advertise the salary.*
13. What characteristics will the successful applicant need for this position?	*This is asking you to match your skills with the job, why you think they are important and what they would bring to the job.*
14. How mobile are you/what do you think of the area/ have you looked at places to live?	*These are questions which indicate your level of interest. Have sensible answers ready.*

Questions to identify your leadership style	
15. How would you describe your work style?	*Do you like to lead, support, control complete tasks from start to finish, investigate, create, etc. Beware – your answer may be tested in role-playing, etc.*

Notes for your response

11.

12.

13.

14.

'Act with confidence'

15.

Potential questions	Observations
16. Do you work well in a team or do you prefer to work alone?	*Remember, this general question will be essential to the job at hand, and clearly if you are not a team player and the role asks for one then this is not the job for you. However, there are many jobs that demand individual focus to succeed.*
17. What irritates you?	*What the interviewer is looking for is your tolerance level – and how well you control your emotional responses.*
18. Give me an example of where you have enjoyed working with other people.	*Just relate any activities that you have been involved in where you felt the collective team had performed well and you enjoyed the experience.*
19. Give me an example of a time when you found it difficult to work with others, and tell me how you coped.	*This can be any team activity where there was a conflict within the team and you were involved. What positive steps did you take to resolve the problem.*
20. Give me an example of where you have taken charge of other people and given them instruction or direction.	*This could be a team-led activity or project where you have had an involvement in its organization and performance.*

Notes for your response

16.
17.
18.
19.
20.

Potential questions	Observations
21. If you were picking a team, what would you look for in the people you would want to select?	*Think about the people you most like working and associating with and why. The likelihood is that you will describe people that best match your own personality and strengths. This is what the interviewer is looking for. Combine your answer with what you believe a team needs to succeed – and the variety of skills involved.*

Questions about your academic experience	
22. Why did you choose to go to college or university, and how did you select the one attended?	*This question has two strands. First, to see if you had thought about your career before entering higher education or whether there were other motives, and secondly, to explore the rationale behind your selection.*
23. Why did you choose the academic subjects you took?	*This is not dissimilar to the question above.*
24. Why did you decide not go to college or university?	*In answering this question there may be as many personal reasons as career reasons. Avoid too much detail; keep it short and positive.*
25. What other activities did you pursue at college or university?	*This question is to establish how you prioritized your time. Were you a loner, a team player, a socialite or a serious student.*

© David Littleford et al. (2004), *Career Skills*, Palgrave Macmillan Ltd

Notes for your response

21.

'Respond with feeling'
22.
23.
24.
25.

Potential questions	Observations
26. How do you think college or university contributed to your development?	*An opportunity to explain how the experience has added to your personal development – do you learn from experiences.*
27. What were the highs and lows of student life?	*You can be slightly flippant here. Student life is to be enjoyed.*
28. Tell us about your academic achievements.	*Be upfront about your grades and if they were lower than you expected, be ready to explain why.*
29. What subjects have you most enjoyed doing?	*Tell them the truth – not what you think they may want to hear – and say why the subject/s were so enjoyable.*
30. What did you least enjoy?	*Again, tell them the truth – and why.*

Notes for your response

26.
27.
28.
29.
30.

Potential questions	Observations
31. What did you think of your tutors and how they influenced your personal development?	*Avoid the temptation to blame the tutor for your short comings. The strength of your response will lie in your achievements. Give praise to good tutors and be proud of your achievements (despite any poor tuition).*
32. How do you think your tutors would describe you?	*Always think of the positive – don't be flippant, and remember you are selling yourself.*
33. Are you currently undertaking any study or training? Do you have any plans for further study?	*This question is looking for your continued interest in self-development. Progressive companies will normally support continuous development but you have to be the driver and commit personal time.*

Questions about you, your attitudes and achievements	
34. What have your main achievements been to date?	*Don't be shy – this is another chance to sell yourself. The response can be any achievement that you are proud of.*
35. Did you win any award, prize or other recognition of achievement, and what for?	*Here they are looking for signs of additional effort, special abilities, dedication, etc.*

Notes for your response

31.
32.
33.

'Don't always jump in with a reply. Give the question some thought.'
34.
35.

Potential questions	Observations
36. Have you any health problems that may limit you from performing the job?	*If interviewers ask this question then they must have a justification as it could be construed as discriminatory. You may respond by saying 'Would it make a difference if I had?' A similar question may be asked of a female as to her intention to start a family. This can also be discriminatory and should be answered in a similar way. Note the response to your question and take it from there. However, ask yourself what you would gain if you did not disclose any health issues you may have. Non-disclosure may cause problems at a later stage.*
37. How would a close friend or partner describe you?	*This needs a lot of thought so prepare well. You will, of course, highlight your strong points.*
38. What motivates you and stimulates your interest?	*Whatever your response to this question, you will need to show real enthusiasm and energy, so think of things where you have had experience that has given you a major buzz.*
39. What de-motivates you and how does that show in your attitudes?	*Think of issues that have affected your enthusiasm to complete a task, and then describe how you have overcome the negative attitudes you felt. Answer in a positive way.*
40. Have you ever been a team leader or held any special responsibilities?	*The interviewer is looking for examples of leadership skills. Remember, this can be any activity you have been involved in.*

Notes for your response

36.

37.

38.

39.

40.

Potential questions	Observations
41. What do you consider to be your major strengths?	*You may have a number, but think of those that can translate into the employer's environment and support your application.*
42. Describe your main weaknesses.	*Think positive and don't let the question move you into a negative mode. Remember that weaknesses can also be strengths, for example being too meticulous, sometimes impatient (because I like to get things done), etc. If you describe a weakness, be prepared to respond with a means to develop and improve the shortcoming.*
43. What do you think are the main qualities for a supervisor or manager?	*This is an opportunity to describe the type of person you would like to work for, who would give you the leadership, support and opportunity to develop. There are many books dealing with management and leadership skills – well worth reviewing to get an understanding. They cover leadership, motivation, control, planning, coaching, counselling and problem solving.*
44. What do you expect to get from a job?	*Here is an opportunity to explore your ambitions and aspirations, both in the short and medium term, in your new career. These should be realistic but don't be afraid to be bold in your targets.*
45. How do you want your career to have developed in five years time?	*Discuss your goals and ambitions but understand that the achievement of your targets will depend on your performance and contribution to the organization.*

© David Littleford et al. (2004), *Career Skills*, Palgrave Macmillan Ltd

Notes for your response

41.

42.

43.

44.

45.

Potential questions	Observations

Questions about your experiences away from an academic environment	
46. Have you been on any unusual or special-interest holidays?	*Looking for the spirit of adventure and curiosity.*
47. Have you been involved in any voluntary or community-related activities?	*If so, explain why and how you were motivated. Your involvement shows a level of social commitment.*
48. What do you do in your leisure time?	*Highlight anything which shows initiative, but don't ignore the 'all work and no play' truism.*
49. Are you a member of any social or civic organization?	*Companies look for closer links with the community at large.*
50. Are you a member of any club? If so, do you serve on the committee?	*This is exploring whether your participation in such activities is passive or active.*

© David Littleford et al. (2004), *Career Skills*, Palgrave Macmillan Ltd

Notes for your response

'Be proud of what you have achieved'
46.
47.
48.
49.
50.

Questions searching for specific competencies	
51. What issues would be faced if a competitor reduced the price of a competitive product/ service drastically?	*The question is looking for you to demonstrate your commercial awareness and to discuss the financial implication of alternative strategies for dealing with the problem. Issues to consider include profitability, market share and people problems.*
52. Your company is relocating to a new site 50 miles away – what are the issues to be faced?	*The main issues behind this question relate to people and how such a move would impact on them. Consider relocation, redundancy or flexible arrangements; the need to retain skills or recruit in the new location.*
53. You are asked to develop a plan for the launch of a new product/service – what needs to be considered?	*Product launches cover all business disciplines from marketing to finance and the question is an opportunity to show your commercial awareness of the issues involved.*
54. You are given a project to run that needs the support of several departments. What skills would you require?	*The competencies needed include planning and organization, team development and leadership, influencing skills, problem solving and communication.*
55. You are given a small team to manage. The average age is 15 years older than yourself and most workers are experienced. What issues will you face and how will you deal with them?	*This is a difficult problem for a young team leader or manager. There could be some resentment and the competencies needed include influencing skills, decision making, communication, problem solving and, essentially, well honed leadership skills.*

Notes for your response

'Distinguish yourself from the rest'
51.
52.
53.
54.
55.

Potential questions   Observations

Use this section to record questions you have been asked...or think you may be asked.
56.
57.
58.
59.
60.

Notes for your response

'Proper preparation gives peak performance'
56.
57.
58.
59.
60.

Potential questions	Observations
61.	
62.	
63.	
64.	
65.	

Notes for your response

61.

62.

63.

64.

65.

Closing questions

Prepare yourself a selection of suitable questions that you will need to have answered in order to make a decision if you are offered the job.

The interviewer will usually give you the opportunity to ask any final questions you may have at the conclusion of the interview.

> Remember, job interviews are a two-way process – you are interviewing the employer just as much as the employer is interviewing you.

However, if the interviewer does not give you this chance then you should ensure that you raise any outstanding points that you may have planned to ask about. Remember that this is your last opportunity before the interviewer terminates the interview to make the assessment of your application.

The types of question that you can ask at this stage, if not already covered, could include:

- What opportunities are there for continued development/training?
- What is the induction process into the company/organization?
- Why has the job opportunity arisen – what happened to the previous incumbent?
- What is the salary and benefit package of the job?

    Many jobs advertise the package associated with the position. Where this is not the case, then it is fair to ask what the package will be. However, the responses may come in several ways, for example:

    - We will deal with pay and benefits at the next stage of interview, should you be selected for the short list.
    - What package are you expecting? – This is the tricky one; a good answer is to state that you do not have a specific figure in mind but would expect the package to be competitive.

- Asking for feedback about your interview (you may wish to be bold and ask if your application meets the requirements of the job).
- What are the next stages following the interview?
- What is the timescale for the decision process?

Always try to ask at least one question before the interview concludes, as most interviewers will doubt that they have answered all the questions you may have. If all else fails, and as a last resort, ask what the company is like to work for.

Learning to relax

In order to present yourself well at interview you must be confident and relaxed, and have the ability to express your ideas with purpose and clarity of both thought and speech.

Speaking outside the familiar background of family and friends, in situations of potential pressure, often causes an unnerving feeling of apprehension that can ultimately act as an inhibitor to free expression. Apprehension shows itself in many guises including heightened nervousness, excess perspiration and a general lack of confidence – the feeling of 'butterflies in the tummy' – that limits your ability to express yourself well. The reaction to this sense of inhibition can often be that you become defensive – the stomach muscles tighten, breathing becomes shallow, the throat dries and feels constricted, the voice becomes less natural – the pitch becomes higher, often with a slight tremor, and you feel you are lacking in control.

The impact on the voice is the most obvious outcome of these symptoms. Remember that your voice is a particularly effective expression of your personality – always try to speak clearly and well, but avoid the temptation to be something you are not – be true to yourself. It would be unwise to try to assume an unnatural tone of voice, accent or delivery – only the highly practised can carry this out with conviction.

There are ways of helping overcome some of the body's natural reactions to stress; being under pressure can cause all the above symptoms. The key to the solution is learning how to control your breathing.

Breathing techniques

Breathing is the most natural function but is largely ignored by most people. Stressful situations affect everyone but the effect can be controlled. For example, actors, presenters and entertainers develop their breathing techniques to significantly enhance their performances. Proficiency in these techniques requires skilled tuition and practice.

However, the basics of breathing techniques can be learnt by following the exercise regime outlined below. These exercises have been designed for you to practise at home. Ideally you should allow yourself ten minutes for each session. Make yourself comfortable, make sure you have a glass of water available and wear clothes that do not restrict.

Exercise 1:   Breathing control
The object of this exercise is to improve your breathing efficiency, and as a result, to give you energy.

Sit comfortably:

- In an upright chair with both feet flat to the floor, hands in your lap, back straight against the chair back with the head in a natural position; don't slouch.
- Relax all the muscles in your body from head to toe – clear any feeling of tension.

Take a deep breath from the diaphragm:

- Place one hand on the lower part of your stomach and the other on your side on the lower part of the rib cage.
- Breath in deeply through the nose and feel the breath naturally pushing your diaphragm downwards (don't force it) into the top wall of your stomach.
- This causes the stomach to move and you will feel it moving outward against your hand; you will also note a movement of the ribs.
- Don't pull your stomach in or heave your chest as you inhale; breath in from the stomach area.
- Over time, the muscles of the diaphragm and surrounding area will strengthen.

Hold the breath:

- For a count of three.

Breath out fully:

- Open the mouth, exhaling slowly and silently in a controlled manner – this ensures that your throat is fully opened and the larynx is not stressed.
- Check that the upper chest and shoulders are relaxed and the head is properly resting; think of a steady stream of air as you exhale.

Repeat:

- As you repeat the process you will begin to feel the movement of your stomach as you inhale and control your exhalation.
- Count out aloud each time you exhale; the number reached will increase as your breathing efficiency improves.
- The exercise should be practised for several minutes and can be repeated as often as you like.
- The more you practise, the quicker you will master the technique and feel the benefit.

Increased awareness:

- It may help if you close your eyes to enhance your concentration level during the exercise.
- Focus on the 'pump action' as your diaphragm strength increases.

- You should become aware of the increased level of oxygen your body is absorbing, and become conscious of a feeling of increased energy.
- Higher levels of oxygenation in the blood improve the brain's efficiency. Controlled breathing encourages relaxation and relieves tension.
- Become attuned with your inner self as your body is energized.

Exercise 2:   Extent of breath

The exercise is intended to give an indication of the increasing capacity of the lungs. Remember that we only speak as we breathe out, and increased lung capacity translates into better control of answers to interview questions.

Use of breath:
- You only speak when you exhale and the object of the exercise is to talk continuously as you exhale.
- Practise Exercise 1 for at least five minutes before you start Exercise 2.
- Talk aloud about anything, or if you prefer, read aloud from a book or magazine, using a single breath – the aim is to use the breath to support your voice over longer periods.
- Time yourself and record your progress.
- Repeat this exercise several times.

Exercise 3:   Relaxation

The objective is to introduce a simple relaxation technique to help control stress and relieve tension. Always make your movements slow and gentle in this exercise.

Shoulders:
- Lift your shoulders very gently and then slowly drop them.
- Repeat several times and each time try to extend the movement; there should be a feeling of ease and awareness of freedom.

Head and neck:
- Gently drop the head forward – pull it up slowly; now allow the head to drop backwards slowly to the full extent of movement, keeping the head in its natural line with the body; slowly return it to its normal resting position.
- Rotate the head slowly to the full extent of movement – once to the left, once to the right – then repeat.
- Be careful to do the above movement 'gently' and be conscious of the movement relieving tension.
- *Do not over-stretch*; always be conscious of what you are doing and how your body is reacting.

Mouth and jaw:

- Exercise the muscles of the mouth, starting with a yawn and stretching the mouth to its widest extent.
- This will feel strange at first but is very effective in relaxing the jaw and making you aware of your facial muscles.
- Practise speaking in an exaggerated manner and notice how the resonance of the voice increases as the mouth opens wider – remember, this is for practice and not for the interview.

Modulation

Control of the voice is an area often ignored. Generally, little time or emphasis is given to voice issues although, ironically, spoken language is one of the fundamental aspects of human interaction.

The combination of voice control techniques, referred to as modulation, is demonstrated in Figure 8.

PITCH + PACE + PAUSE + POWER = PERFORMANCE

Pitch: The level of tone in the voice; higher tones indicate stress, whilst lower tones usually indicate a relaxed, confident attitude, but could also be dull.

Pace: The speed and timing with which an answer is given: a rapid-fire response often indicates lack of confidence and can cause confusion, and too slow a response is equally bad – the issue here is one of reasonableness; the delivery will ideally be conversational and confident, matched with appropriate content.

Pause: Suitable pauses indicate to the listener that you are considering your words with care; pauses also assist in giving emphasis to the points raised; and, as with pace, the correct use of pauses adds to the appreciation of your comments rather than detracting from them.

Power: The strength of the voice must be appropriate to the circumstance of the interview or presentation; think about the space between you and the interviewer – you need to 'fill the space' with your voice.

Figure 8 Modulation

All trained athletes and sportsmen practise their skills regularly and, in particular, warm up thoroughly before a race or contest. The exercises are designed to help you practise the rhythm of your breathing and develop your vocal skills at the same time, to empower you in the interview situation. Preparation helps you control your nerves, frees you from the worst effects of stress and enables you to perform to the optimum.

Exercise 4:   Listen to your voice
The objective is to give you practice in answering questions while you listen to your own voice. Use of a tape recorder will be helpful although not essential.

Performance practice:
- Practise speaking for one minute on any topic; this will give you experience in both thought formation and planning 'on the hoof'. Listen to your voice as you deliver your comments.
- Use emphasis and modulation for variety and impact.
- Be conscious of the resonance of your voice: resonance increases the fullness of the voice, adding interest, richness and vocal colour.
- Avoid quoting the number of specific points you want to make in an answer; you may forget the later ones – creating unnecessary stress.
- Select questions from the model questions earlier in Step 4 and deliver answers as if you were in a live interview; this will enable you to listen to your voice as well as checking the content of your answers.
- Devise a list of other tasks to perform, such as summarizing a recent newspaper article or television programme.

Critical assessment:
- Assess yourself on the modulation, clarity and construction of your answers, together with the confidence of your delivery.

Before the interview

Work out an exercise regime that you can practise prior to the interview. Realistically this will be a briefer set than your normal home-based exercises. Find a place to sit quietly and go through your relaxation routine.

Think about shoulders – head – breathing – relaxing the jaw and the face muscles by stretching them. Use your breathing techniques as you go into the interview room to act as a calming influence and to enhance your blood oxygen levels.

It is a good idea to take a small bottle of water with you – to lubricate and freshen your mouth and throat; wear clothes that do not restrict you and always leave yourself time to prepare.

Confidence comes from knowing that you have prepared well and that you are able to express yourself with truth and conviction. Respect the interviewers, but also respect your own contribution – you cannot be other than who you are. Be the best that you can be and make sure they see the real you.

Interview rehearsals

Interviews, as we have said, can be nerve racking if you are not properly prepared. A great way to get ready is to have a couple of 'dry runs'. Check your network of contacts and see if anyone would be happy to give you interview practice – in fact a couple of rehearsals. These first rehearsals will help you tell if you are clear in the sort of answers you have prepared. Your dummy interviewer may throw in a couple of new questions you need to work on.

Do it properly, seriously, as if you were in a real interview. Get the interviewer to give you honest feedback about your performance. What was good, what was bad, what sounded honest, what sounded unconvincing? At the very least it is invaluable experience; at its best it can get you out of a sticky situation in a real-life interview.

Practise, practise and practise again. Record yourself – most audio units have microphones built in and tapes are inexpensive. If you can, use a video camera or equivalent to highlight issues of body language – posture, fidgets, eye contact and so on. Refer to Step 5 – Communication tools. Practise, review your presentation and work on the obvious errors highlighted.

> *The will to win is important . . . but the will to prepare is vital.*
>
> Joe Paterno (US football coach, born 1924)

Step 5

Communication tools

The single biggest problem in communication is the illusion that it has taken place.

George Bernard Shaw (1856–1950)

The ability to communicate effectively forms a key part of the process you are undertaking in your job search, whether you are face to face, on the telephone or writing to a potential employer. To communicate well you need to develop and practise core skills in:

- active listening (content and tone of voice);
- observation (of body language, gestures, etc.);
- speaking (in a manner appropriate to the listener);
- writing (using language that is clearly understood by the reader);
- interpretation of the written word (for example, the content of an advertisement);
- creating an environment where two-way contact can be maintained.

This Step will give you a quick review of the techniques involved in effective communication – the 'active ingredient' in your formula for success.

- Communication is an instinctive skill.
- Methods of communication are many and varied.
- We are involved in some form of communication throughout the waking day – whether verbal or non-verbal.

Most people, if asked, will say that they believe they communicate well. However, in reality their understanding of communication may not be complete. People often 'inform' or 'tell' but fail to listen to the response or reaction. The language they use may mean different things to different people and this can prevent two-way contact being established or maintained.

We all take our communication skills for granted and are pretty sure that we are good communicators. If someone doesn't understand what you are saying, then whose fault is it – yours or theirs?

At its basic level communication is a simple concept, but because even the smallest emphasis on a word can change the sense of a phrase, in reality it is hugely complicated. We often don't realize the impact that we have on other people – both in a positive, but especially in a negative way.

Communication is used to produce the results we want, but does it always work as we intended? There are often misunderstandings, instructions are not followed, relationships are affected, morale falls, grudges are created, self-confidence and efficiency suffer.

To be an effective communicator you need to recognize and develop the skills that actually bring about the results you want. Effective communication calls for a whole range of specialized techniques . . . but the good news is that they are all easily picked up and developed.

Communicating effectively

'Communication' is the way in which we exchange information between one another, and, because we are mortal beings, it is influenced by feelings, prejudices, perceptions and attitudes.

For communication to take place, information has to flow in two directions – that is, the 'receiver' picks up the message from the 'sender' and confirms receipt by giving some form of recognizable feedback – even if it is no more than a gesture (a grunt seldom qualifies as good feedback). Without *real* feedback you cannot be certain that communication has in fact taken place.

For communication to take place effectively your message has to be received as you intended – and not misinterpreted. Do you remember how, at school, the best teachers continually questioned students to check and confirm the level of understanding of the subject being taught? *Did you ever play the game of Chinese Whispers?*

Communication is a complex process, taking place both verbally and non-verbally in a whole variety of ways:

spoken word	body language
gestures	written word
facial expression	pictures
emphasis on words	tone of voice
signs	choice of language
emotional reactions (flush, blush, etc.)	

Communication is not simply the act of telling (and *that* will probably come as a big surprise to a lot of people). It is a highly complex process made up of several defined 'elements', which depend on each other for success. The elements which apply to you as 'the sender of the communication' are:

- **Content:** The information that you want to pass on.
- **Delivery:** The method you use – word of mouth, letter, etc.
- **Style:** Your use of language and words, the tone of your voice, facial expressions, gestures, etc.
- **Attitude:** The manner you adopt – a message delivered with confidence is more likely to be believed.
- **Judgement:** Your perception of the attitudes and abilities of your 'audience' – don't underestimate them.
- **Listening:** Receiving the feedback from the communication so that you can measure its success.

If the 'style' contradicts the 'content' you will cause confusion and misunderstanding. Flippant comments or inappropriate statements may antagonize the receiver (especially if an interviewer), and your communication will have failed to achieve its purpose. The success of any communication depends on all the elements being in harmony.

The success of any communication is gauged by the understanding of the receiver. This can only be measured by the feedback given. You need to be prepared to listen carefully to hear the messages sent back to you – and ask for feedback if it is not given. If you are not interested in the feedback given, you will lose valuable information and could be seen as rude or arrogant. Beware – it is all too easy to turn off your listeners.

Written communication

This area of communication is, in some ways, more difficult than any other form of communication in that you leave a permanent record in the hands of the receiver. This can be recalled without contradiction at any time – so choose your words wisely and with great care.

We have already covered, in Step 2, the significance of good presentation, layout, construction and the use of meaningful words. Only use words that you understand and that are non-offensive.

When you read what you have written, consider whether the content can be misconstrued in any way. This is the one form of communication that you may not get meaningful feedback from. *Always* keep a copy of every document you issue.

Listening

Listening is not simply 'hearing' – it is the fundamental skill of receiving and interpreting messages with all your senses. Hearing only picks up sound vibrations, whereas listening picks up all the signals transmitted – both verbal and non-verbal.

A communication will be effective if the intended message is the one that is actually received. In face-to-face communication the skilled listener will give undivided attention to the sender, and will:

- listen without prejudging or forming conclusions too early;
- ask questions to clarify the meaning;
- focus attention on the speaker and keep eye contact without staring;
- avoid unnecessary interruptions (and especially 'hijacking' the conversation);
- show that the comments made are valued (never dismiss the views of another);
- summarize to check understanding of the content.

Listening is a skill which most people take for granted, but is often dramatically under-developed. Sadly, there are very few truly natural communicators (albeit there are millions of people who are convinced they are). Good communicators must be good listeners. Skilled listening requires focus, patience, tolerance and a high degree of intense concentration. When used properly, listening enables the receiver of any form of communication to achieve the correct understanding of the meaning of the message.

> *We have two ears and one mouth so that we can listen twice as much as we speak.*
>
> Epictetus, Greek philosopher (AD 55–135)

Body language

What do we mean by body language?

'Body language' is the term used to describe most forms of physical movement of any part of the whole body that communicates messages, either consciously or subconsciously, in a non-verbal form to anyone who is within eye range.

It is extremely powerful, and work in this field demonstrates the effectiveness of body language as a component part of presentations:

Content of the message	7%
Tone of voice used to deliver the content	39%
Body language of the presenter	54%

The message is clear – people listen with *both* their eyes and their ears.

Experience shows that the style of delivery (that is the overall performance) has the most significant impact on the listener. Messages are also greatly enhanced by the presenter varying the tone of voice to emphasize aspects of the content.

These skills are naturally generated by enthusiasm and self-belief in what you are saying.

> Enthusiasm beats boredom – a bored interviewer doesn't hear what you are saying.

Another important aspect to consider, linked to body language, is style of dress – the clothes worn and how they are worn (being untidily dressed may create a negative impression). What you are wearing may divert the listener's attention from what you are saying.

Body language becomes particularly relevant for you in an interview situation. Handshakes, eye contact, stance, sitting posture, clothes, all become strong influences on the interviewer.

Movement and position of the body, and alterations to the pitch and tone of voice, can also indicate interest or heightened awareness; for example, facial expressions and leaning forward can indicate increased interest.

Unsighted people will be more sensitive to verbal indicators and in particular to alterations in the tone and pitch of the voice – the manner of delivery as well as the content. Deaf people will be more sensitive to body language than those who have all of their physical senses available to them.

The results of poor communication

The results of poor communication can be quite dramatic. They range from simple misunderstandings to offence, antagonism, and harm to personal image which may not be recoverable.

Once you have offended or upset someone it will take a lot of hard work and effort to make good the damage. Just think back to discussions and arguments at home, or amongst your friends – communicating badly is much easier than communicating well. As a starter, in the words of a home-spun philosopher, 'engage brain before opening mouth or putting pen to paper'. Emails can be devastating – like the written word, they cannot be retrieved once sent.

Barriers to effective communication

There are many barriers to effective communication, and listed in Table 1 are some examples of the typical causes, and the effects which result from them.

Table 1 Barriers to communication

Cause	Effect
Confused message	Unstructured or badly planned messages have little chance of success as the listener will often be confused and most likely misled.
Bad delivery	Poor, confusing or inconsistent delivery will also probably result in misunderstanding, or even the message being ignored.
Jargon and language used	Badly chosen words are one of the major causes of poor communication. The words used need to be suitable to the message and appropriate for the audience. Incorrect words can create anger, offend, upset, intimidate or destroy credibility.
Selective hearing and reading	We only hear what we expect or choose to hear – we only read what we expect to see. Everything else is ignored, which can seriously damage your prospects of selection for a job (before or after the interview).
Arrogance	Ignoring instructions or information which conflicts with what we believe can be a highly effective barrier to communication.
Emotion	Our emotional state conditions our attitude of mind. You will not listen or respond appropriately if you are in a temper, have been insulted or are emotionally upset.
Word blindness	Words mean different things to different people. Use of the wrong word loses or distorts the message and ultimately devalues the sender.
Tedious topics	Be sensitive to the listener's reaction on topics that may have little interest or appeal. Attention will begin to wander and parts of your message will be lost.
Poor concentration	Failure to listen can result from lack of concentration, distractions or preoccupation with other issues (such as formulating your answer before the interviewer has finished speaking).

Put it into practice

The most important thing in communication is to hear what isn't being said.

Peter Drucker, author and consultant (born 1909)

It is really very simple. Good communicators are willing to learn the skills involved and continually fine-tune them.

Listen to yourself and others, listen to your friends, analyse conversations and reports on radio and television. Try out the different communication techniques. Go over past misunderstandings and arguments to identify what actually caused them and how you influenced the outcome. Analyse and review communications that you are currently involved with. Observe good and bad speech patterns. Identify practices that worked well and those that failed for future reference. Only use jargon if your audience will understand and appreciate the meaning – but never use slang expressions.

Work at it, you can only measure your results by feedback or lack of it. Continue to practise to improve. Don't be afraid to try something different. Learn from your experience – if you don't experiment it will be difficult to improve and you may miss opportunities to influence people.

Success at communication only comes from experience coupled with a clear understanding of the processes involved. Once the skill is learned it becomes an automatic behaviour – a life skill for success.

Step 6

The interview

No one can make you feel inferior without your consent.

Eleanor Roosevelt (1884–1962)

This is where all the hard work you have done in preparing yourself is put into practice. Interviews are experiences that you should enjoy – and not fear.

Prepare for the interview

Having been notified of the interview there are several tasks you must complete:

- Confirm acceptance of the interview appointment, time and place.
- Be certain that you know where you are going and plan to have plenty of time to get there.
- Check your travel arrangements to make sure there are no problems on the day.
- Review your CV – remember what you have written.
- Collect any documentation you have been asked to take with you or that you think may be useful (spare CVs, certificates, evidence of qualifications, written references, etc.).
- Don't find out on the day of the interview that your clothes are in the wash or at the cleaners.

Disabilities

The disclosure of any disability is the choice of the individual. Not to disclose a disability, whether asked to or not, could put the candidate at a disadvantage during the interview process. Individuals with physical constraints on mobility may need provision for suitable access to buildings and toilet facilities. An individual who is blind may need a designated guide and/or arrangements for a guide dog. Ultimately, knowledge of such requirements will enable the organization to make suitable arrangements to avoid delay or putting the candidate under unnecessary stress.

Where the disability is not obvious, such as deafness, partial or colour blindness and dyslexia, disclosure helps the interviewer to make provision for any specific requirements. With certain forms of dyslexia, for example, it may be easier for the individual to complete forms and questionnaires or take tests on a PC rather than in written form.

The day of the interview

Interviews can be stressful experiences so do what you can to reduce the tension. Expect to be nervous, which is no bad thing as you will be alert – being too relaxed and 'laid back' may convey a lack of interest or enthusiasm, and could lead to over-confidence.

- Go with the intention of enjoying the experience.
- On no account be late.
- Make sure you have time to compose yourself before the interview (and have a comfort break).
- Practise your relaxation exercises (see Step 4).
- Be polite to everyone (including the Receptionist – making a good impression makes you feel good).
- Switch off your mobile telephone.

The best laid plans can be disrupted by circumstances beyond your control, so have a contingency plan – have the interviewer's telephone number with you and make contact *before* the scheduled time for the interview explaining the problem. If you have to leave a message with someone make sure you take a note of their name and the time you called.

How to approach the interview

Remember that the interview starts the moment you meet the interviewer (or his/her colleagues), without a word being spoken. The following basic guidelines will help you create a positive impression:

- Visual presentation (dress sense, hair, fingernails, jewellery, cleanliness) will convey an unspoken statement to the interviewer – good *or* bad.
- Be confident in your manner and friendly in your approach.
- Protocol – take a lead from your introduction – that is, the way the interviewer greets you: 'Hello Mr/Miss Jones my name is Andrew Brown', refer to him as Mr Brown; if the greeting is 'Hello Steven/Sharon, my name is Andrew Brown', refer to him as Andrew.
- Positive body language – use good posture, smile, keep eye contact, don't fidget (or play with a pen, etc.), avoid too much use of hand movements or folding your arms (a defensive/protective stance), use a firm handshake (not a bone crusher).
- Maintain rapport with the interviewer by mirroring their body language – lean forward.

- Demonstrate your energy through the tone and pitch of your voice – sound interesting and not monosyllabic.
- Speak clearly – don't gabble; don't use slang or 'easy speak'.
- Don't interrupt – only respond when the interviewer has completed the question/statement.
- Only use words where you know their meaning.
- Don't be adversarial – you can disagree without being aggressive.
- If you have a strong belief, speak with passion, but do not impose your views on the listener – other people are entitled to their views.

First impressions set the scene – build on them.

During the interview

Interviews are 'living things' and all are different. You will have to respond to everything thrown at you, but these guidelines will help you keep focused and give a high-quality performance:

- Interviews are a two-way process – you are interviewing the employer as much as the employer is interviewing you.
- Keep full concentration throughout the interview – don't daydream.
- Look interested and not bored.
- Note-taking during the interview: most interviewers don't mind but it is courteous to ask first.
- Handling silence – some interviewers will deliberately leave a 'pregnant pause', usually after you have answered a question. Don't fall into the trap of filling the silence with unnecessary waffle. Stop when you have completed your answer.
- Answering questions – 'engage brain before opening mouth' (give yourself thinking time – you can use facial expression to indicate thought processes).
- Keep your answers focussed and to the point without being too short; lengthy replies can switch off the interviewer and shorten your time to shine.
- If you are unsure of the interviewer's meaning, qualify the question.
- Don't pontificate, preach, crawl or creep.
- Don't be flirtatious or over-play your social skills.
- Don't patronise the interviewer – you may be academically highly qualified, but the interviewer influences decisions about who gets the job.
- If the interviewer has a strong accent, resist any temptation to mirror it – this could be seen as mimicking or being patronizing – in any event, it can easily cause offence.
- Listen to what the interviewer actually says – not what you think he or she is saying.

- If you are offered a drink during the interview, take it if you feel you may need to lubricate your throat to avoid it drying.
- If you accept a drink be careful not to spill it – a spillage could cause a distraction and damage your confidence.
- Be ready for anything.

Obviously you want to get a job and that is your prime consideration. However, at this stage your objective should be to come out of the interview knowing that you have done your best.

> **Referring to your CV**
> It is acceptable to refer to your CV and supporting documentation during the interview. However, there is a risk that you could disrupt the flow of the interview and possibly give the impression that you are uncertain about the details of your background and experience – something about which you should be an expert.

Come out satisfied that you have performed well and that you have enjoyed the experience. You should be prepared to assess your performance objectively and realistically. If you feel you could have done better then learn from it. As soon as possible after the interview, record your thoughts, highlighting any areas of your performance that you feel need improving – use the interview assessment form, which can be found later in this Step (Figure 10).

All interviews depend on the personal chemistry between interviewer and interviewee. Unfortunately not all interviewers are professional or well trained, and some may have extraneous pressures on them that have nothing to do with you or the interview. Providing you leave the interview with the feeling that you have given a good account of yourself you can, quite rightly, feel satisfied with your performance.

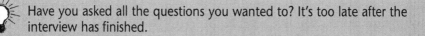 Have you asked all the questions you wanted to? It's too late after the interview has finished.

Types of interview

- Formal interviews are usually well structured and maybe on a one-to-one, panel, or group basis. Where there are several interviewers, treat them all with the same level of respect. This is because the person controlling the interview in a panel situation may not be its most influential member. Maintain eye contact – address the speaker but don't ignore other members of the panel.

● Informal interviews may be arranged on a 'come and have a chat' basis. Whilst this means that the atmosphere will be more relaxed it does not mean that you should concentrate less or let your guard down. All interviews, whether formal or informal, must be treated with the same principles of conduct, preparation and seriousness.

Interviewers have feelings and prejudices

The list in Table 2 shows examples of verbal and non-verbal characteristics of applicants that can have a significant influence on the attitude and perception of the interviewer. The list is not exhaustive but covers the majority and should help you to prepare well.

Interviewers' questioning techniques

Step 4, 'Your Interview Tool Kit', includes sample questions which you will have reviewed prior to the interview. There are several ways that questions may be asked and you have to consider how to respond. To be fore-warned is to be fore-armed.

Open questions invite you to do most of the talking to describe an opinion, a view or a situation. For example, 'What skills would you bring to the company?'

'Fishing trip' questions are of a general nature, where the interviewer is looking for an avenue to explore that may put you under pressure. For example, asking your opinion on a political issue of the day. Your response should be measured and considered and not give way to high emotion or total disinterest – otherwise the interviewer may exploit the response as a potentially negative attribute of your personality. This is not to say that you should not be passionate in what you believe, but you should pick the ground and use it to your benefit.

Probing questions are used after an open or 'fishing trip' question to start a discussion, which usually prompts further questions to find out more about you. For example, 'I am interested in your views on . . . Can you tell me more?'

Leading questions are questions asked that imply the answer. For example, 'Don't you agree that . . . ?' Treat these with caution as they could be traps – always be true to yourself.

Closed questions are either limiting questions that only seek to verify information, or badly worded questions where a 'yes/no' answer could be given.

Table 2 Positive and negative influences

'Turn ons'	'Turn offs'
• Maintaining high energy levels.	• Showing low energy, poor posture, and being too casual.
• Showing enthusiasm.	• Behaving badly – bad manners, rudeness, lack of respect.
• Being reasonably respectful.	
• Having a neat/tidy/clean appearance and good dress sense.	• Arriving late.
• Being punctual.	• Lacking knowledge of the company/organization/products/services.
• Demonstrating obvious interest in the opportunity.	• Being inadequately prepared for interview.
• Showing knowledge of the company/organization.	• Lacking concentration; being easily distracted.
• Demonstrating good listening skills by paying attention.	• Having a patronizing attitude; being arrogant, underestimating the interviewer.
• Speaking clearly and giving coherent replies.	• Asking a question when the information has already been given.
• Having good manners – being polite and not discourteous.	• Making platitudes; being condescending.
• Using non-verbal body language – smiling and maintaining good eye contact (not staring).	• Lacking humour; being pedantic.
	• Having poor personal hygiene, for example unkempt hair, dirty fingernails.
• Maintaining concentration (ignoring distractions).	• Being untidy in appearance, wearing dirty shoes.
• Having a good sense of humour (but keeping it under control).	• Dressing too casually.
• Making paperwork available – certificates, spare CVs, references.	• Lacking eye contact.
	• Interrupting the speaker.
• Confirming that the logistics of the job have been considered – location, access, etc.	• Ignoring the logistics of the job/location/access.
	• Giving poor, ill-considered answers.
• Using language correctly and with understanding.	• Asking irrelevant or badly constructed questions.
• Asking pertinent and well-constructed questions.	• Waffling; not knowing when to stop; being too verbose.
	• Using words badly and incorrectly – using slang; talking too quickly if nervous.

However, try to avoid the temptation to answer with 'yes' or 'no' where you feel you can develop an answer that puts you in a good light and provides the interviewer with relevant information.

Most frequently used questions, that is, those that are almost guaranteed in one form or another, will refer to your Strengths and Weaknesses. The 'strengths' question is easy – you cover what you are good at. It is the 'weaknesses' question that can expose your frailties, therefore be prepared for the question by responding with a perceived weakness that could be seen as a strength. For example, 'I find it difficult to tolerate bullies and racists' or 'I sometimes spend too much time on detail'. It is not wrong to explore weaknesses but they can quickly lead you into giving a negative impression. Be careful and be well prepared.

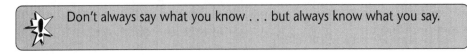

Don't always say what you know . . . but always know what you say.

How to handle questions that you consider to be discriminatory

Questions posed by an interviewer regarding the following could almost certainly be considered as discriminatory:

- your state of health;
- disabilities;
- plans for a family;
- race;
- religion;
- political beliefs;
- sexual orientation.

You are entitled to ask why the question is being posed, but do so in a non-confrontational way.

- Unfortunately your response may be seen as confrontational by the interviewer.
- If you feel that the purpose of the question was discriminatory you should state your concerns and refrain from answering the question.
- Note the interviewer's response – if the interviewer is genuine he/she will try to recover the situation.
- Decide, after the interview, if you feel that you have been discriminated against and what action, if any, you feel appropriate.
- If you decide to pursue your concerns, however, be clear that you are acting for the right reasons and not as revenge for not getting the job.

Be very careful – don't look for discriminatory questions, but if you are convinced there is one, politely ask the purpose of the question.

Assessment centres – role-play, presentations and psychometric testing

Larger organizations often use assessment centres when recruiting at graduate level or for specialist skills. The sessions normally last at least a day and allow the recruiting organization to assess candidates in a variety of situations, over a prolonged period. Candidates benefit because they can be assessed over a series of tasks that have to be performed rather than simply being judged on a single interview.

In graduate recruitment programmes a large proportion of organizations employing in excess of 500 staff use preliminary screening techniques based on electronic application forms. These forms are designed to be completed by candidates via the Internet, and are scored according to the competencies required by the employer. They are based on questionnaires with multiple-choice answers and can include control questions. They may also incorporate timed ability tests.

The screening process identifies candidates to be taken to the next stage of the recruitment process, and candidates will then be asked to provide their CVs. Candidates can expect to be re-tested on their responses to the questionnaire to ensure consistency and to check the honesty with which the questionnaire was answered.

Normally, if a battery of tests is to be used at an assessment centre, applicants can ask for sample practice material to familiarize themselves with the format, and most organizations will provide it.

The following techniques can be used in assessment centres:

- interviews;
- role-play;
- presentation;
- aptitude tests – for example, testing creative thinking/numeracy/logical thought;
- academic tests (written papers);
- personality assessments.

The principal objectives are to bring together a group of candidates at one time, giving the organization the opportunity to observe candidates in both individual and group interactive situations. Candidates will be assessed as individuals in personal interviews, and will also be assessed as part of a group. The group will be set tasks which mirror work situations, providing the observer with the opportunity to assess individuals' performances, identifying their skills in leadership, team participation, communication, planning, use of time, priority setting, etc.

Groups will often have the chance to mix socially with the management team in an informal situation, probably over a meal. Although this is intended to be relaxing you should be careful not to let your guard down. Where the assessment takes place over two days, ensure that you behave appropriately in the evening – do not over-indulge in alcohol or food. Whilst 'Big Brother' may not be watching, you can be sure you will be noticed. Normally the dress code will be advised and will be casual – don't interpret 'casual' as being untidy.

Act normally, but remember that you are being constantly assessed and also bear in mind that 'No input; no impact'.

The format of a typical assessment centre will include some or all of the following elements:

Introduction session
An informal introductory session allowing you to meet fellow candidates, the selectors and representatives of management. You will be given details of the process to be followed.

- Remember, the assessment process starts immediately you arrive at the assessment centre.

Information session
An information session giving details about the company or organization. You could be given the latest data about the company/organization.

- You may well need this information during the course of the assessment.
- You can compare this new information with the research data you already have, to develop possible questions at interview.

Group tasks – role-playing
Group tasks involve some form of role-play to solve problems and will typically be based on the use of team work to deal with situations or problems faced by an organization or business. Each individual will be given a brief, and you should read it carefully to understand the task that is required of you and of the group. Sometimes the brief will be general and the roles not assigned to individuals; the group will resolve the allocation amongst themselves.

The aim of the exercises will be to identify the various individual skills and personalities of the candidates and assess how they will build or integrate into a work team.

The assessors will be looking for your contribution to the team, and your skills in communicating, planning, logical thought, leadership skills, etc. The exercise can be stressful and your reaction to that stress will be monitored.

- Assess information given as quickly as possible.
- Identify your objectives, establish priorities and develop a strategy.
- Be assertive, diplomatic, persuasive and tactful – remember that you are working in a group and your objective is to demonstrate both your team and individual skills.
- Act normally, don't overplay your role – over-acting and insincerity will show through.
- Listen to other people's opinions; be constructive but not dismissive.
- Keep the task and timescale in focus, keep your cool and do not lose your sense of humour.
- Always be active and not passive. State your views clearly. Do not sulk if you don't get your own way.

Group tasks – practical
The group may be asked to use equipment or materials to construct something, for example drinking straws and toy bricks to make a bridge. The selectors are more interested in the group's interactions than the finished product. They will assess planning, problem solving, creative thinking and application.

- These tasks can sometimes appear to be silly and pointless but enter into the spirit of the exercise, show enthusiasm and try to enjoy it.
- You will need to use many of the skills outlined in the 'Group tasks – role-playing' section shown above.

Act normally, get involved . . . and remember, 'No input; no impact'.

Aptitude and academic tests
As mentioned earlier, these may be given online prior to the event and will then be repeated at the assessment centre. They will be timed and controlled under examination conditions. The tests are designed to measure the intellectual capability to use logical and analytical reasoning, and also your proficiency in the core skills of maths and English.

The tests are measured against a notional national norm for the group being assessed. Practice papers will usually be available on request. Most tests will be of a multiple-choice nature.

- Read instructions carefully.
- Ask for clarification if you are unsure.

- Work quickly but accurately.
- Where questions offer multiple-choice answers and you are undecided on which to select, make an educated guess and return to the question if you have time – always give an answer, as you have a chance of getting it right.
- Some of the questions will involve mathematics – make sure that you are prepared for this (you may not be allowed the use of a calculator).
- There are a number of publications providing examples of these types of test – use these to practise, especially the core skills of maths and English (if your confidence needs a boost).

Personality questionnaires

These questionnaires are not usually timed and there are no right or wrong answers. They will ask you to decide how you would react in different situations and some questionaires will ask you to select a preference from a range of alternatives. Your responses will help identify the type of role most suited to you.

Remember that personality questionnaires will only confirm what you already know about yourself.

- Read the instructions carefully.
- Answer the questions honestly – if you don't, the way the questions are formatted will highlight an inconsistency; it is extremely difficult to manipulate the results.
- It is best to put down your initial reaction to each question rather than trying to anticipate what the 'correct' answer may be.

Presentations

Presentations may be required as part of the assessment and can involve the group as a whole, or in teams, with individual contributions.

If individuals are required to make a short talk or presentation it is normal for prior notice to be given so that appropriate preparations can be made in advance.

You will be given a limited time and you should make full use of it, covering all the points you wish to make.

- Your audience will appreciate clarity – don't be too detailed or technical.
- Use notes as a prompt, avoid reading from a script as this will inhibit your delivery.
- Keep eye contact with your audience and not just one individual.
- Talk to them – not at them.
- Put your watch in easy view and don't overrun.

- Speak clearly and project your voice; don't rush, gabble or mumble.
- Don't be too serious – however, avoid funny stories or jokes to illustrate points. Use the colour of your voice for emphasis.
- Use body language to animate your presentation – keep your head up, avoid excessive use of the hands and creating barriers by folding your arms, etc.
- Practise the presentation, ideally in front of a colleague, to gain confidence, check timing and get feedback.
- If you are using visual aids don't obstruct the audience's view. Talk to the audience not the aid.
- Use of flip charts – if your spelling is weak keep it simple; write clearly so that all your audience can read the content.
- If you are stuck, remember the old adage as a fall-back position:
  'Tell them what you are going to tell them.'
  'Tell them.'
  'Tell them what you have told them.'

Note:
You may be required to make a personal presentation at an interview. You may be given a topic or be allowed to choose a subject. Normally you will be advised of this requirement in advance, giving you time to prepare. However, this is not always the case as some interviewers may be interested in your ability to cope, faced with a real surprise. If you are given a free choice, select a topic of general interest that you are both familiar and confident with, and on which you are able to answer questions. Avoid jargon or technical terminology not easily understood.

Summary

In any assessment centre the key objectives are to participate and contribute to the activities that employers use to make their final selection. By doing so you have the opportunity to leave the interviewers with a positive impression of your abilities, personality and potential. You will be assessed on how you perform within the set tasks and interact with other participants. The assessment centre provides the opportunity for assessors to validate candidates' competencies against the criteria required by the roles that are being filled.

By nature assessment centres are competitive environments and you will need to think on your feet. They are good opportunities to learn about the culture and plans of an employer and the relationship it has with its employees.

 Being yourself carries far less risk than trying to be something you are not. It's the real you they want to see. Remember, the assessment is about you – the topics are secondary.

CANDIDATE ASSESSMENT (underline as appropriate to the candidate)

Responses to questions
Clear/unclear
Well structured/muddled
Comprehensive/adequate/insufficient
Irrelevant information
Quick/slow to respond

Words chosen well/poorly
Easy/difficult to follow
Rambling
Hesitant/confident
Rash/thoughtful

Voice
Confident/nervous
Clear/mumbled
Fast/normal speed/slow

Normal/forced
Loud/normal level/quiet
Enthusiastic/monotonous

Posture
Upright/slouched
Attentive/uninterested
Aggressive/passive

Tense/relaxed/nervous
Confident/uncertain

Gestures
Expansive/normal/restricted
Excessive use of hands

Fidgeting

Facial expressions
Natural/forced
Enthusiastic/uninterested
Conflicting with words

Lifeless/expressive
Nervous/relaxed

Eye-contact
Normal/staring/avoiding

Distracted/attentive

Attitude and manner
Sincere/insincere
Relaxed/nervous
Shy/confident/over-confident
Enthusiastic/uninterested
Assertive/passive/outspoken
Serious/normal/flippant
Involved/distant

Convincing/unconvincing
Agreeable/irritating
Lack of confidence
Natural/forced
Open/defensive
Argumentative/controlled
Rash/thoughtful

Questions asked by applicant
Rash/thoughtful
Muddled/well structured
Well researched/lacks interest

Intelligent/irrelevant
Confident/rambling
Too forceful/hesitant

Figure 9   Candidate assessment

A sample interviewer's candidate assessment form

The candidate assessment form shown in Figure 9 is the type that any interviewer could use. It is simply aimed at helping the interviewer judge your performance. Look at yourself under each category and decide how you would rank yourself – assess yourself after each interview.

Interview self-assessment form

We have provided a form (see Figure 10) that you can use after each interview. The form has been designed to analyse the interview and your performance (good or not so good), and to make notes to help you to develop your interview techniques. The form is of particular benefit if you are called back for a second or short-list interview. A copy of the form to photocopy from is provided in Appendix 4.

Interview assessment form

Complete this form as soon as possible after your interview (be honest!).

Company/organization:

Location: Date:

Name of interviewer/s:

Was I on time?	Yes / No	Was I confident?	Yes / No
Were my answers clear?	Yes / No	Was I relaxed?	Yes / No
Was I enthusiastic?	Yes / No	Was eye contact good (not staring)?	Yes / No
Did I speak clearly (not gabble)?	Yes / No	Did I waffle?	Yes / No
Was my posture good?	Yes / No	Was I well mannered?	Yes / No
Did I sound coherent?	Yes / No	Did I fidget?	Yes / No

What did I do well?

Tricky questions:

Was my research good enough? If not, why?

Anything I could have done better?

Ideas for the next interview:

Overall:

Did I enjoy the interview?   Yes / No   Did I do my best?   Yes / No

What happens next?

Figure 10   Interview assessment form

Telephone interviews

There is an increasing trend amongst larger companies and organizations to use telephone interviews for initial pre-selection before applicants are called to attend personal interviews.

The normal procedure is for the company, having received your application, to send an application form to you, either by email or letter, for completion and return. You will be asked to specify contact numbers and convenient times for the interviewer to call should your initial application be accepted.

This type of application form often includes wide ranging questions and these can give a fairly clear idea of the questions you are likely to be asked over the telephone. The questions will be designed to highlight the specific competencies needed by the company or organization and also give indicators of your strengths as a prospective employee – for example, your personality, practical experience, motivation, style in a working environment, temperament and overall potential.

When the first contact is made it is usual for the interviewer to explain the key areas that will form the basis of the interview and to arrange a time when it will be convenient for the telephone interview to take place. Ensure that you have been given a contact number for the interviewer in case there are any last minute hitches with the arrangements.

As part of your preparation for the interview, review your responses to the model questions contained in Step 4 – Your Interview 'Tool kit', and check your answers to the questions in the application form. Have your CV available.

Make sure that you have some time, prior to the call, to relax, gather your thoughts and steady your nerves.

It is essential that you treat this interview in exactly the same way that you would if you were face to face with the interviewer. Tips on telephone techniques are given in Step 2 – Your Personal Sales 'Toolkit' under the section 'Telephone Job Applications or Enquiries'.

Try to keep your responses succinct and to the point, maintain a confident tone, don't get flustered, and if you can't answer a question, don't fudge a reply.

Be prepared for silences that may occur after you have responded to a question – sometimes it may appear that the interviewer is no longer on the line. Remember that interviewers occasionally leave pauses to see if you will fill them – avoid the temptation and don't waffle; simply stop talking when you have answered the question. Of course, you should check if you feel that the line has really gone dead – if it has, wait a while for the interviewer to call you back before you try to make contact.

With telephone interviews you can only judge the feedback you are receiving by the tone and pace of voice. Don't be lulled into a false sense of security by a casual approach from the interviewer; this may encourage you to relax your guard and become too informal. Don't be too exuberant in your approach but do be friendly, good humoured, interested and forthright.

Remember, when you can only communicate verbally, your voice is the key asset in getting your image through to the interviewer. The tone, pitch and pace of your voice, in delivering your message, creates the first opportunity for the interviewer to develop a personal impression of you.

When asked if you have questions, at this stage restrict yourself to enquiries about the process. Detailed enquiries about the job, remuneration packages, company style and so on, will be dealt with later at the more formal stages. However, at the end of the interview, do make sure that you establish when you are likely to hear the outcome.

Telephone interviews are only the first step in the process of selection and will always be followed up by face-to-face interviews and/or assessment centres for successful candidates. Remember that the impression you create on the telephone will need to be sustained at the subsequent interview/s.

Second or short-list interviews

Preparation
It is important that you complete your interview assessment form immediately after your initial interview. Reviewing your responses and overall performance, together with any issues that came up during the process, gives a solid foundation in preparing for the next step.

A second or short-list interview means that you performed well, and that the interviewer considered that you were a suitable candidate for the job. The competition now gets tougher – there may only be one vacancy.

The first question you need to ask yourself is whether the job is actually what you want, and if it were offered, whether you would accept it. If not, now is the time to consider refusing the invitation politely – to avoid wasting time. To continue with the interview without the intention of accepting the role if it were offered could put you in a bad light should you want to join that organization in the future.

You will have obtained sufficient information during the first interview to identify areas for further research into the organization and its operations. You may have some outstanding questions that need answering before the next interview – phone up and ask.

You may be asked to prepare new information, or make a presentation (refer to the notes on Presentations earlier in this Step).

Remind yourself of the disciplines outlined at the beginning of this Step, covering preparations for the initial interview.

The interview
Second interviews will usually mean you will meet new people and face more in-depth questions. You cannot rely on the relationship or connections made with the initial interviewer, and even if the previous interviewer is present, still maintain a courteous and professional approach. You could be introduced to staff as a potential future colleague, and have an opportunity to view the full working environment. If this takes place before the interview, be prepared to convey your thoughts, reactions and observations.

Also, the interview may introduce tests or a different assessment format. If it is a panel interview, remember to try to embrace all of the panel members in your answers and avoid isolating any one person (the quiet one may actually be the decision maker).

The type of question you may face could include:

- Now that you have had time to think about the role you will have some additional questions or comments – would you like to share your thoughts with us?
- What attracts you to our organization?
- If offered the job, would you accept it?
- Where do you see yourself and the organization in the next five years?
- If asked to travel or relocate would that give you a problem?
- Who do you think are our major competitors?
- What are our major opportunities?
- What have you found out about the organization since your last visit?
- What do you think are our major products, goals, aspirations or strategies?
- What expectations do you have of our organization?
- How ambitious are you – and what motivates you?

Be clear about your expectations from the organization in terms of remuneration, benefits, short- and medium-term career prospects. Don't be too forceful but equally don't be too shy – strike a balance.

Case studies

Case study 1

Peter had applied for a position in the legal department of a multinational organization, and had been short-listed through the UK company's sifting mechanism for final interviews with two levels of management. Each of the planned interviews was carried out by functional and line-management personnel.

The first-level interview was conducted by the European Functional Head (female) accompanied by the UK Personnel Manager (male). Between the two it was decided that the Personnel Manager would take the lead role and this enabled the Functional Head to observe and ask searching technical questions.

Peter was correctly introduced to the interviewers and made aware of their roles, seniority, and responsibilities within the organization. At the start of the interview Peter displayed a high degree of confidence with a touch of arrogance; he was self-assured and obviously very competent. However, during the course of the interview it became increasingly clear that he felt that the male Personnel Manager held control and was most influential. His body language made this obvious; he moved his body position towards the Personnel Manager to the point where his shoulder and legs pointed directly towards him, thus shielding Peter from the Functional Head. This became even more pronounced, to such an extent that all answers given by Peter, irrespective of who actually put the question, were addressed to the Personnel Manager. Whilst it was assumed that Peter's actions were subconscious, they were nevertheless very obvious and both interviewers were disturbed by his attitude, as they found it disrespectful and insensitive to the senior member of the interview panel.

The next-level interview was with the UK Chief Executive, to whom the job ultimately reported, and the Director, to whom the European Functional Head reported – both were male. This interview went well and both interviewers were impressed with his background, competence and presentation skills.

The interview panels had agreed to review the outcome of all of the interviews jointly, to reach a consensus decision on whom to appoint. Sadly the damage had already been done and Peter was not appointed.

Peter made four basic misjudgements in his first interview:

● He ignored protocol – the roles and seniorities had been clearly explained to him.

- His attitude was seen as patronizing and arrogant.
- He failed to include both panel members in his responses.
- His negative body language alienated both panel members.

Case study 2

Latifa was keen to obtain a position as a graduate trainee with a local authority following her graduation with an Honours degree in Economics and German. She had applied to a number of authorities and was delighted when invited to an initial interview for a large county council. Before the interview she carried out considerable research into the authority, checking local press, technical journals and websites, and additionally she asked her father for advice. His network included a colleague who had held a senior position within a local authority and clearly understood its organization, role and structure. Latifa was introduced to him and he advised her that there were six key areas that he felt questions could be asked about, to test her research and understanding. These potential questions were clearly of a more general nature than those related to the profession she had chosen.

- What is the population of the county?
- How many districts and boroughs are there within the county?
- What is the difference between a district and a borough council?
- What are the main towns in the county?
- What are the main industries and businesses in the region?
- Are there any Government initiatives that impact on local authorities?

The questions identified additional areas of research and as a result she became confident in her ability to respond to them in detail if asked. At the interview she presented herself well and during the interview four out of the six questions were raised in one form or another. Latifa was able to respond authoritatively and at the end of the interview she felt that she had accounted for herself well. On returning home she contacted her father's colleague to give him feedback and to thank him for his help and guidance.

Latifa was called back for a second interview; this also went extremely well and as a result she was offered the job. As part of the feedback from the interview panel they expressed their delight in her initial responses and the fact that she had obviously researched the authority well and taken time to understand some of the issues they faced. Her father's colleague continues to be part of Latifa's growing network and she keeps him updated on her progress and development.

What worked towards Latifa's success?

- Knowing the career she wanted to follow.
- Researching the organization she was being interviewed by in depth.

- Using a network contact (albeit not her own) to advise and assist.
- Further research into the additional advice given.
- Being able to give a confident, knowledgeable and accomplished presentation at interview as a result of her research and preparation.
- Maintaining her network after the event.

Case study 3

Roger was not clear what career path to follow having graduated with a general degree in social sciences. However, he was fortunate that his father was well connected in the City and was able to arrange for Roger to have an informal chat with a contact who was the Chief Executive of a major finance house.

As it had been set up as an informal chat, Roger viewed the meeting casually and thought that the Chief Executive might help him to decide on a suitable career.

Roger had failed to realize that people of this seniority are extremely busy and their time is valuable. Amongst other searching questions, he was asked to outline what he knew about the company, what value he would bring and what were his specific skills. Roger had made no attempt to prepare, and, therefore, could not provide any suitable or convincing responses. After a courteous 30 minutes the meeting was terminated; the Chief Executive wished him well with his future job search but was unable to offer any further assistance.

It is obvious that Roger wasted a priceless opportunity:

- He failed to recognize that any meeting regarding careers should be treated as an interview.
- He was not clear what he wanted to do or properly prepared for the meeting.
- Not researching the company and its products left him badly exposed and could also have been seen as discourteous.
- He left a poor impression of himself, which could be remembered.
- Calling upon his father's network and performing badly could have caused embarrassment to his father. (Use networks properly – don't abuse them.)

Case study 4

An international company was looking to recruit a student to take part in an environmental project lasting over the summer vacation period. If the student proved to be suitable at the end of the project, the company planned to offer a position in its management development programme.

Invitations were issued to several students who had contacted the company on an 'on spec' basis and also some who had replied to an advertisement run in several environmentally supporting journals.

Teegan was an Australian graduate now completing a second degree in this country where she had family and was able to obtain the necessary permits to work. Her style was very open and outspoken verging on being forceful. She was passionate about environmental issues, and had campaigned as a contributor to several fieldwork projects in Australia.

She had previous interview experience where she had been short-listed on several occasions without success. Feedback indicated that, whilst she had lots of passion, her style was seen to be too assertive, tense and outspoken and, on occasions, her enthusiasm stopped her listening to the interviewer.

Teegan discussed this feedback with her friends, family and tutors. The consensus was that her enthusiasm was a key strength, but that she should consider controlling her delivery without losing the passion for her beliefs. She was also given several pointers about the standards of behaviour, attitude and approach expected of job applicants.

One of her friends also pointed out that when she became stressed and tense some blushing occurred on her neck and upper chest. This is quite a common response to emotion or pressure and is easily covered by garments with high necklines.

Armed with this advice Teegan was able to modify her style. She prepared herself to adapt to the different cultural requirements, practised hard and controlled her normal instinctive responses in order to listen more effectively. She also enrolled on a relaxation course.

The company invited her to interview and she was ultimately selected for the project. Her performance was exceptional and she was also offered a placement on the management development programme.

Teegan's success was helped by the following factors:

● She was confident enough to ask for advice from tutors, friends and family.
● She demonstrated her ability to adapt to cultural differences.
● She was able to develop her listening skills which improved her ability to respond more effectively and with controlled passion.
● She learnt and practised relaxation techniques which helped to reduce stress and tension.

Step 7

After the interview

When one door closes, another opens, but we often look so long and regretfully upon the closed door, we do not see the ones which open for us.

Alexander Graham Bell (1847–1922)

Assess your performance

We have provided a self-assessment form (see Figure 10 in Step 6) for you to complete after each interview. The form allows you to measure your performance at the interview and identify what went well, what you felt could be improved, together with various other observations. Completing the form immediately after each interview will have more value as the experience will be fresh in your mind, but be objective in your comments to get maximum benefit.

Review the opportunity

After the interview you should take time to consider all of the points raised, the details of the job, benefits and development opportunities, and to be clear whether, if the job is offered to you, you would take it. If 'yes', the waiting process begins. If 'no', then a polite phone call or letter explaining that you would like to withdraw your application is best done now rather than later.

If you are being considered for more than one job and all of them appeal, then it would be sensible to do a critical analysis of all the pros and cons of each job so that you can make a considered judgement. In reality you may not be able to conclude this until you have firm offers of employment showing full details of all the packages.

Waiting for the outcome

It is always difficult to predict the outcome of an interview unless the interviewer has given you a very strong indication that you are likely to receive a job offer. However, from experience, you should be aware that nothing is certain until you actually receive a formal offer in writing. This forms the first basis of a contract.

The period between interview and decision can be tense – not unlike waiting for exam results. There is little you can do until the date the interviewer indicated that you would receive notification. If you have not heard by that time it would not be unreasonable to make contact and enquire as to the outcome of your interview. There are many reasons why the timescale may have extended, almost always due to internal circumstances within the company or organization. The delay will normally only affect those candidates who are being seriously considered.

Those who have definitely been unsuccessful are normally notified quite quickly. It is also not unusual for companies and organizations to delay a decision where they have more than one strong candidate. The reason behind this is that if their first choice does not accept an offer, they will re-offer to their reserve candidate. Remember the saying 'sometimes no news is good news'.

If you have been successful you will receive a written offer detailing your remuneration package and giving you the terms and conditions of your employment. Sometimes initial notification will be by telephone, but you should only rely on the written offer as this gives you the full details of the contract.

Accepting or rejecting the offer

If you have any queries about the offer you should clarify them prior to acceptance. It may be that you feel the package offered is not attractive enough and you want to negotiate an improvement, or that you want further clarification on some of the key points discussed at the interview.

Ensure that you are clear about any changes you are looking for and how determined you are that those changes are essential. You have to balance any short-term gain against the longer-term opportunities that will be available. If they are not essential then your approach should be low key and non-confrontational: for example, 'Is there any opportunity to improve the offer?'

If an improvement is essential, then be prepared to walk away from the offer.

Your acceptance or rejection of the offer also should be in writing, but it would be courteous to convey your decision initially by phone.

If you are rejecting the offer, be prepared to give genuine reasons for the rejection and don't be surprised if the company or organization try to persuade you to reconsider your decision.

Always remember to thank them for the offer and time taken. Remember that politeness costs nothing and you may meet the interviewer again in the future. Don't forget our advice on networking.

If you are in the fortunate position of having several offers, make sure that you have considered all of the facts before making your final decision. Once you have accepted an offer you have in fact entered into a contract. To reverse your decision afterwards, without good cause, may limit your chances with that organization in the future.

An unsuccessful application

To be turned down is always deflating, even if you half expected the result. It is even more difficult to handle if you feel that the interview process was very positive and promising.

Unfortunately there are fewer jobs than applicants, and it is not always easy for the employer to make a final decision when 'spoilt for choice'.

You may decide to contact the interviewer and ask for feedback about your interview, and in particular, advice on areas for improvement. Some interviewers will respond genuinely giving you objective comments, but the majority will use catch-all phrases like 'it was a difficult decision because there were so many strong candidates' – this will probably be true.

Remember that every step taken is a new experience that you can learn and develop from. Don't get despondent, and keep on applying.

If at first you don't succeed, try, try again.

W. E. Hickson (1803–70)

The next step

Working on the principle that you have not put all your eggs in one basket, one rejection is not the end of the world. You will now turn your attention to the other applications that you have made, or have yet to make, in your search for employment.

Continue the process detailed in this workbook and accept that there is a job out there waiting for you – all you have to do is keep looking for the right one.

 You've got to keep going to get anywhere.

Step 8

Into the future . . .

Formal education will make you a living; self education will make you a fortune.

Jim Rohn (US motivational speaker and author)

Starting work

You will, no doubt, have a mixture of excitement, apprehension and nervousness when you start work. However, you will have experienced some of these feelings in the process of getting the job in the first place. The hard work you have put into achieving your success will continue – but now you get paid for it.

It is impossible to predict what you will find when you join a company or organization but the following guide is representative of good practice. You may be going straight into a designated role, or into a defined training programme where you will experience different roles over a given period. In either case it is most unlikely that you will be 'dropped in at the deep end' without proper induction or training.

Most companies and organizations have an initial induction programme for new employees. These will vary in length from half a day upwards. The intention behind the process is for you to meet your new colleagues and to be provided with information which gives you a clear understanding of:

- the company or organization, how it is structured, its standards, rules and goals;
- your role and where you fit into the company or organization;
- what is expected of you, how your performance will be measured and by whom;
- health, safety and environmental standards;
- training and development opportunities;
- the facilities available to you – for example, canteen, staff purchases, sports club, etc.

Don't be too disappointed if your induction training is side-tracked by pressure of work. Most organizations will complete the process but not in the structured way intended by them.

Joining the team

Any organization has rules that are mandatory and form part of any employment contract. These are normally laid out in the details provided with your formal offer of employment.

There are also informal rules and standards of acceptable behaviour expected of you. From our experience it is better to start off with the right approach and attitude. Whilst the points below are not mandatory they provide a quick guide to help you fit into your new team successfully. They are a foundation from which you can develop principles for your working life and are intended to help you avoid the pitfalls and traps that can easily be fallen into by the unwary.

- Meet all the conditions of your contract, for example timekeeping, attendance, confidentiality, disciplinary code, health and safety.
- Contribute to the team effort in all tasks, including the menial ones.
- Meet objectives set, including the timescales – if in difficulty raise issues before deadlines.
- Be respectful but not subservient.
- Recognize knowledge and experience in others – don't be a 'know it all'.
- Continue to develop your listening and communication skills.
- Recognize the dress code of the company or organization.
- Keep your own counsel and don't be too trusting – you are now entering a political business world, where people have their own agendas.
- Avoid becoming entrapped in the 'office politics'.
- Be good humoured – be ready for 'leg pulling', which will be well meant.
- Treat people at face value unless they demonstrate that they are not sincere.
- Be principled – have the courage of your convictions but be ready to learn the art of compromise.
- Always act honestly, with integrity and within the law.
- Own up to your mistakes and don't compromise others.
- Learn from your mistakes – you will make them, and if identified early enough they can be rectified – but don't make the same mistake twice.
- Avoid horse play as this can have serious and dangerous consequences.
- Avoid any form of harassment or discrimination – such action will contravene the disciplinary code.
- Ask questions if you are unsure, and keep on asking until you understand the answer.
- If the company or organization offers a mentoring system (a manager who is given the task of supporting you), use it wisely and never abuse it.
- Treat people with respect and consideration (remember, you are always networking); you may need their help or support in the future.

- Where constructive criticism is given, accept it with good grace and use it in your personal development.

Communication structures

All organizations have both a formal and an informal structure. The formal structure is traditionally based on the management hierarchy, where managers know their respective positions within the organization. The informal structure is based on the 'grapevine', where information is passed on within the workforce in an unofficial but highly effective and rapid manner. You cannot avoid being touched by this process – however, you can and should avoid the risk of being party to it. Avoid gossip and tittle-tattle – one of the biggest generators of unproductive and wasted time

Enthusiasm is the electricity of all businesses and organizations.

Conclusion

The knowledge and experience you will gain from using these Steps will support you throughout your career. Keep the Steps, working papers and completed forms together with your own notes and records for future reference. They will serve as an invaluable base point with which you will be able to review and compare your personal development through the early stages of your career.

You can update your original responses to the questions and issues raised within this workbook as your experience grows through lifetime learning, knowledge and any further educational achievements.

The older you get the more you know you don't know.

Anon

The step-by-step approach has taken you through the process of achieving your first career job, and will be equally valuable for your next and any further job changes. The underlying principles and techniques focus on you, helping you identify what your goals are and how you can achieve them.

A final thought . . .

If you are in the penalty area and don't know what to do with the ball, put it in the net and we'll discuss the options later.

Bob Paisley (1919–96), Manager of Liverpool Football Club

Appendix 1

Style notes

Fonts and margins

Font style   Use a business-like serif typeface such as Times New Roman.

Font size   12 point (11 point can be used to avoid a letter running
                  on to 2 pages).

Margins   ● Top: your letter should start at least 2.5 cm below your
                    address (see below for layout).
                  ● Left and right: 2.5 cm each.
                  ● Bottom: 2.5 cm.

Layout

Letter headings   Use your word processor to develop a personal letter
                  heading. Use a different font (for example a sans serif
                  such as Arial) and a smaller font size. Look for an
                  aesthetic balance in the alignment of the letter and letter
                  heading.

Justification   All letters should be left aligned or fully justified – see
                  examples in Appendix 3.

Length   Wherever possible, keep letters to a maximum of one
                  page.

Date   Dates appear as the first text line of a letter. The date
                  precedes the recipient and is separated from it by a blank
                  line. Show the date in full – numbers and words (for
                  example, 30 June 2004).

Recipient   The recipient should be addressed as 'Mr', 'Mrs' or 'Ms' –
                  'Esq' may be used following the name if preferred. Job
                  titles should always be used *and* make sure they are
                  correct.

Address   Postcodes are always used.

Salutation   Separate the last line of the address from the salutation
                  by three blank lines (this may be reduced to two lines if it
                  avoids the letter running to two pages, or increased to
                  four in short letters). Always try to write to a named

	person and use their name rather than 'Dear Sir' or 'Dear Madam' (for example, 'Dear Mrs Brown'). Avoid using first names as this could be seen as too familiar.
Text	Separate the text from the salutation by one blank line. Split the text into paragraphs where appropriate and separate it from other paragraphs by a single blank line. This makes your letter easier to read and improves the appearance.
Punctuation	Punctuation can be omitted from address details and endings of letters (for example, commas at the end of address lines, 'Yours faithfully', etc.). However, main text paragraphs should be properly punctuated.
Endings	Separate the endings of letters ('Yours . . .' etc.) from the text by a single blank line.
Signature space	The standard signature space is 5 blank lines – this can be reduced to 4 lines if space is limited.
Writer's name	Clarify your marital status in brackets if you are female and your name could be male or female, or if you are only using initials, otherwise it will be assumed the writer is a male. For example Chris Duffy (Miss) or C. Duffy (Ms).
Enclosures	Put 'Enc' if there is one enclosure, 'Encs' if more than one.
Envelopes	Make sure the envelope is addressed correctly and clearly, showing the postcode. It is acceptable to mark the envelope to safeguard confidentiality, e.g. 'Private and Confidential', 'Strictly Private and Confidential', 'To be opened by Addressee Only'.

Style

Paper	Use good quality paper (at least 80 gsm) but avoid strong colours. This applies equally to your CV.
'Faithfully' or 'sincerely'	'Yours sincerely' is only used in letters addressed to a specific person (e.g. Dear Mr Smith). Letters addressed to 'Dear Sir' are always concluded with 'Yours faithfully'.
Affectionate terms	Terms such as 'Kind regards' should only be used where the recipient is well known to the writer.
Bullet points	Be careful not to mix bullet point styles – use bullet points, numbers or letters – but not a mixture.

Common mistakes	• Do not shorten words or phrases – use 'have not', *not* 'haven't'; 'should not', *not* 'shouldn't'.

Common
mistakes

- Do not shorten words or phrases – use 'have not', *not* 'haven't'; 'should not', *not* 'shouldn't'.
- Link 'should' with 'would' (e.g., 'I should be grateful if you would . . .'), and 'would' with 'could' (e.g., 'it would be very helpful if you could . . .') – *never* 'would' with 'would'.
- Avoid long sentences – they are difficult to follow and can be confusing. Split long sentences into 'bite-sized chunks'.
- Read the letter before you send it – and read the words you have actually written, *not* the words you *think* you have written.
- Avoid slang, and abbreviations not in general usage.
- Apostrophes should always be used correctly, for example 'the project's objectives' (where project is singular) or 'the projects' objectives' (where more than one project is referred to).
- Nouns which are singular are sometimes mistakenly thought to be plural. For example, company names are singular so 'Smith Ltd' should be referred to as if it were a person, not as a group of people – so, 'Smith Ltd has introduced . . .'.
- Never address a letter to 'Dear Mr Fred Brown' or 'Dear Mr F. Brown' – you see this often where mail merges are carried out from databases.

Word power

All words are powerful. Therefore, be sure you understand their meaning in their context. They can also convey your style (see Step 5, 'Communication tools').

Emphasis

Use bold type, capital letters or underlining as a means of emphasis. Use one of the three options only, and not in combination (for example, don't underline capital letters).

Spelling and grammar

Spelling

If in doubt, check the spelling (dictionaries are wonderful things!). Always make doubly certain that you spell names correctly. People can get quite upset if you do not spell their names correctly – it also indicates a lack of research.

Remember you are trying to impress, and if you see a mistake in your letter, re-print it (or write it out again). Once a letter is posted it is out of your hands and cannot be recovered.

When using word processors make sure that you are using a British dictionary file – US spellings can be significantly different, e.g. colour/color, labour/labor.

Spell checkers are very useful but are not intelligent – they check the word not the meaning – there is no substitute for reading you work (blame the computer at your peril – we did in fact mean '**your** work').

Grammar   Proper use of direct/indirect object (me).

Examples: 'John and I visited . . .' but 'Thank you for visiting John and me . . .' (To check for sense read the phrase without the reference to the other person – that is, 'I visited . . .' , 'Thank you for visiting me . . .'.)

Avoid using unnecessarily long words for effect – they make meanings harder to comprehend and rarely impress.

Be careful not to repeat words in single sentences as this could indicate a lack of vocabulary or imagination.

Punctuation should be checked carefully as it can significantly change the meaning of a sentence. If unsure it is probably better to omit it – 'If in doubt, leave it out.'

If in doubt about a phrase or sentence try rephrasing it – this is usually effective and it often actually makes the sense of your letter clearer.

Watch out for the use of the word 'however'. This word is best used at the start of a sentence rather than as a joining word (as a conjunction). It carries more impact and focuses on the positive rather than lingering on the negative.

Never start sentences with conjunctions such as 'And' or 'But' unless you are intending to make a strong point. Otherwise it could indicate poor sentence construction.

Grammar is a huge subject and if you are unsure about any issues, you should consider purchasing one of the many books on the subject.

Appendix 2

Sample curriculum vitae layouts

On the following pages are four examples of different CV layouts. As we have said earlier, there is no right or wrong way of presenting your CV. The presentation is very much an issue of your personal preference and what you feel portrays the best image of you to potential employers.

Note the use of white space in the examples and how the air of clean, uncluttered efficiency improves the overall effect. The content is, of course, down to you.

Always tell the truth on your CV – not that you wouldn't anyway! However, always stress the positive.

Remember that most employers will check the critical items you show (exam grades, achievements, work experience, etc.), and there are now even specialist agencies that will carry out this task for employers.

Your mission is to produce a CV to be proud of, one that pleases you every time you look at it and read the content.

If at all possible, have it produced on a word processor and printed by a good quality printer. This is simply because it is so much easier to change word processed documents than those typed or handwritten, and the standard of presentation is much better and more professional. Always use the best quality paper you can get. We would suggest you resist the temptation to use folders or special bindings as these will actually inconvenience the person reviewing an applicant's CVs.

Your CV is your personal advertisement – make sure the content and presentation is nothing less than excellent.

CURRICULUM VITAE

Name:	Roger Peter SMITHSON
Address:	10 Goodby Avenue
	Upton
	Anytown
	AX4 2ZX
Telephone:	0111 222 3456
Email:	roger.smithson@people-perf.co.uk
Date of birth:	21 November 1981
Marital status:	Single

I am a highly motivated, confident and enthusiastic graduate with an aptitude for written and verbal communication. Since graduating I have acquired a basic grounding in business management techniques within the media distribution industry. I have excellent computer skills and am looking for a stimulating and challenging position that will give me the opportunity to make a real and meaningful contribution.

EDUCATION

1999-2003	**University College Anytown**
	BA (Hons) Business Studies and Law, Class 2.1
	This specialised business course expanded my awareness of business management skills and law. The course covered the disciplines of sales, marketing, accounting and information technology, and involved a four-month work assignment with a marketing consultancy. My dissertation explored diversity within developing SMEs.
1997–1999	**St Leonards College, Anytown**
	Sixth form college 'A' Levels

1 – Grade A
2 – Grade B

1992–1997	**De Montfort High School, Anytown**
	GCSE:
	GNVQ:

5 – Grade A
4 – Grade B
2 – Distinction

I was awarded school colours in cricket, rugby, drama and swimming and captained the school cricket team.

KEY SKILLS

- Excellent verbal and written communication skills
- Strong interpersonal skills
- Computer literate – Word, Excel and PowerPoint
- Languages: French (fluent); German (conversational)
- Highly numerate
- Team player with proven leadership skills
- Full driving licence

EMPLOYMENT

2004   **PNP Promotions**

Since graduating I was given a short-term contract to work with the Agency assisting with a project creating and delivering shareholder information for a major PLC.

VACATION JOBS

2002–2003   **PNP Promotions**

Promotions Assistant – This was a four-month placement and I gained experience of general promotional activities, advertising, administration and creative development work. I was subsequently given the chance to do vacation work with the Agency and the experience gained has been the major reason behind my choice to work in the media.

1999–2001   **Anytown Advertiser**

Reporter (vacation work) – This was my first experience of working in the media, and working as a trainee reporter taught me how to source and tailor stories to the specific target audience. It was also my first experience of working in a highly pressurised and time-sensitive environment. Three of my articles were published.

1998–1999   **Hornbeam House, Anytown**

Volunteer – This work involved caring for mentally ill residents and the organisation of various therapeutic group activities. The residents were all young adults.

1997–1998   **Anytown Social Services**

Ambulance Guide – The role of this position included care work for severely mentally ill patients during transport to and from special care centres. I was also actively involved with patient care and the organisation of group activities at the centres.

PERSONAL INFORMATION

At university I was a member of the film-making club and wrote regularly for the in-house magazine. I enjoy film and drama, comedy, literature, music and most sports, playing at football at weekends. I also enjoy travelling (both this country and abroad) and experimenting with vegetarian cookery. I am passionate about environmental and conservation issues and do voluntary 'hands-on' work for the Footpaths and Walkways Association.

REFEREES

Mr David Davidson Tutor, University College Anytown,
The High, Anytown AX1 1AA.
Telephone: 0111 101 2321.

Mrs Jocelyn Jones, Director, PNP Promotions,
PNP House, Grange Drive, Anytown AX1 3ED.
Telephone: 0111 199 5555.

PERSONAL PROFILE

Name:	**Roger Peter SMITHSON**	Marital status:	**Single**
Date of birth:	**21 November 1981**	Nationality:	**British**
Address:	**10 Goodby Avenue**	Driving Licence:	**Full**
	Upton		
	Anytown AX4 2ZX		
Telephone:	**0111 222 3456**		
Email:	**roger.smithson@people-perf.co.uk**		

EDUCATION

1999–2003   **University College Anytown**
BA (Hons) Business Studies and Law, Class 2.1
This specialised business course expanded my awareness of business management skills and law. The course covered the disciplines of sales, marketing, accounting and information technology, and involved a four-month work assignment with a marketing consultancy. My dissertation explored diversity within developing SMEs.

1997–1999   **St Leonards College, Anytown**
Sixth form college 'A' Levels   1 – Grade A,   2 – Grade B

1992–1997   **De Montfort High School, Anytown**
GCSE: 5 – Grade A,   4 – Grade B
GNVQ: 2 – Distinction

I was awarded school colours in cricket, rugby, drama and swimming, and captained the school cricket team.

SKILLS

I am a highly motivated, confident and enthusiastic graduate with an aptitude for written and verbal communication. I have excellent interpersonal skills and am highly numerate. I am fluent in French with conversational ability in German. I have proven leadership skills and am a dedicated team player. Since graduating I have acquired a basic grounding in business management techniques within the media distribution industry. I have excellent computer skills and am looking for a stimulating and challenging position that will give me the opportunity to make a real and meaningful contribution.

PERSONAL INFORMATION

At university I was a member of the film-making club and wrote regularly for the in-house magazine. I enjoy film and drama, comedy, literature, music and most sports, playing at football at weekends. I also enjoy travelling (both this country and abroad) and experimenting with vegetarian cookery. I am passionate about environmental and conservation issues and do voluntary 'hands-on' work for the Footpaths and Walkways Association.

EMPLOYMENT

2004   **PNP Promotions**
                Since graduating I was given a short-term contract to work with the Agency
                assisting with a project creating and delivering shareholder information for a
                major PLC.

VACATION JOBS

2002–2003   **PNP Promotions**
                Promotions Assistant – This was a four-month placement and I gained experi-
                ence of general promotional activities, advertising, administration and creative
                development work. I was subsequently given the chance to do vacation work
                with the Agency and the experience gained has been the major reason behind
                my choice to work in the media.

1999–2001   **Anytown Advertiser**
                Reporter (vacation work) – This was my first experience of working in the
                media, and working as a trainee reporter taught me how to source and tailor
                stories to the specific target audience. It was also my first experience of
                working in a highly pressurised and time-sensitive environment. Three of my
                articles were published.

1998–1999   **Hornbeam House** (Anytown)
                Volunteer – This work involved caring for mentally ill residents and the
                organisation of various therapeutic group activities. The residents were all
                young adults.

1997–1998   **Anytown Social Services**
                Ambulance Guide – The role of this position included care work for severely
                mentally ill patients during transport to and from special care centres. I was
                also actively involved with patient care and the organisation of group activities
                at the centres.

REFEREES

Mr David Davidson, Tutor, University College Anytown,
The High, Anytown AX1 1AA.
Telephone: 0111 101 2321.

Mrs Jocelyn Jones, Director, PNP Promotions,
PNP House, Grange Drive, Anytown AX1 3ED
Telephone: 0111 199 5555.

CURRICULUM VITAE

Name: Roger Peter SMITHSON
Address: 10 Goodby Avenue
             Upton
             Anytown
             AX4 2ZX
Telephone: 0111 222 3456
Date of birth: 21 November 1981
Marital status: Single

EDUCATION

1999-2003 **University College Anytown**
BA (Hons) Business Studies and Law, Class 2.1
This specialised business course expanded my awareness of business management skills and law. The course covered the disciplines of sales, marketing, accounting and information technology, and involved a four-month work assignment with a marketing consultancy. My dissertation explored diversity within developing SMEs.

1997-1999 **St Leonards College, Anytown**
Sixth form college 'A' Levels: 1 – Grade A, 2 – Grade B

1992-1997 **De Montfort High School, Anytown**
GCSE: 5 – Grade A, 4 – Grade B
GNVQ: 2 – Distinction

I was awarded school colours in cricket, rugby, drama and swimming, and captained the school cricket team.

I am a highly motivated, confident and enthusiastic graduate with an aptitude for written and verbal communication. Since graduating I have acquired a basic grounding in business management techniques within the media distribution industry. I have excellent computer skills and am looking for a stimulating and challenging position that will give me the opportunity to make a real and meaningful contribution.

KEY SKILLS

- Excellent verbal and written communication skills
- Strong interpersonal skills
- Computer literate – Word, Excel and PowerPoint
- Languages: French (fluent); German (conversational)
- Team player with proven leadership skills
- Full driving licence

EMPLOYMENT

2004   **PNP Promotions**
              Since graduating I was given a short-term contract to work with the
              Agency assisting with a project creating and delivering shareholder
              information for a major PLC.

VACATION JOBS

2002 2003   **PNP Promotions**
              Promotions Assistant – This was a four-month placement and I gained
              experience of general promotional activities, advertising, administration
              and creative development work. I was subsequently given the chance to do
              vacation work with the Agency and the experience gained has been the
              major reason behind my choice to work in the media.

1999 2001   **Anytown Advertiser**
              Reporter (vacation work) – This was my first experience of working in the
              media, and working as a trainee reporter taught me how to source and
              tailor stories to the specific target audience. It was also my first experience
              of working in a highly pressurised and time-sensitive environment. Three of
              my articles were published.

1998 1999   **Hornbeam House** (Anytown)
              Volunteer – This work involved caring for mentally ill residents and the
              organisation of various therapeutic group activities. The residents were all
              young adults.

1997 1998   **Anytown Social Services**
              Ambulance Guide – The role of this position included care work for severely
              mentally ill patients during transport to and from special care centres. I was
              also actively involved with patient care and the organisation of group
              activities at the centres.

PERSONAL INFORMATION

              At University I was a member of the film-making club and wrote regularly
              for the in-house magazine. I enjoy film and drama, comedy, literature,
              music and most sports – I play at football at weekends. I also enjoy
              travelling (both this country and abroad), experimenting with vegetarian
              cookery and I am concerned about the environment and its conservation.

REFEREES

              Mr David Davidson, Tutor, University College Anytown,
              The High, Anytown AX1 1AA.
              Telephone: 0111 101 2321.

              Mrs Jocelyn Jones, Director, PNP Promotions,
              PNP House, Grange Drive, Anytown AX1 3ED
              Telephone: 0111 199 5555.

ROGER PETER SMITHSON

Address: 10 Goodby Avenue
                Upton
                Anytown
                AX4 2ZX
Telephone: 0111 222 3456
Email: roger.smithson@people-perf.co.uk
Date of birth: 21 November 1981
Marital status: Single

I AM A HIGHLY MOTIVATED, CONFIDENT AND ENTHUSIASTIC GRADUATE WITH AN APTITUDE FOR WRITTEN AND VERBAL COMMUNICATION. SINCE GRADUATING I HAVE ACQUIRED A BASIC GROUNDING IN BUSINESS MANAGEMENT TECHNIQUES WITHIN THE MEDIA DISTRIBUTION INDUSTRY. I HAVE EXCELLENT COMPUTER SKILLS AND AM LOOKING FOR A STIMULATING AND CHALLENGING POSITION THAT WILL GIVE ME THE OPPORTUNITY TO MAKE A REAL AND MEANINGFUL CONTRIBUTION.

KEY SKILLS

- Excellent verbal and written communication skills
- Strong interpersonal skills
- Computer literate – Word, Excel and PowerPoint
- Languages: French (fluent); German (conversational)
- Highly numerate
- Team player with proven leadership skills
- Full driving licence

EDUCATION

2003–   **University College Anytown**
           BA (Hons) Business Studies and Law, Class 2.1
           This specialised business course expanded my awareness of business management skills and law. The course covered the disciplines of sales, marketing, accounting and information technology, and involved a four-month work assignment with a marketing consultancy. My dissertation explored diversity within developing SMEs.

1997–1999 **St Leonards College, Anytown**
           Sixth form college 'A' Levels   1 – Grade A,   2 – Grade B

1992–1997 **De Montfort High School, Anytown**
           GCSE: 5 – Grade A,   4 – Grade B
           GNVQ: 2 – Distinction

           I was awarded school colours in cricket, rugby, drama and swimming, and captained the school cricket team.

EMPLOYMENT

2004   **PNP Promotions**
              Since graduating I was given a short-term contract to work with the Agency
              assisting with a project creating and delivering shareholder information for a
              major PLC.

VACATION JOBS

2002-2003   **PNP Promotions**
              Promotions Assistant – This was a four-month placement and I gained
              experience of general promotional activities, advertising, administration and
              creative development work. I was subsequently given the chance to do
              vacation work with the Agency and the experience gained has been the major
              reason behind my choice to work in the media.

1999-2001   **Anytown Advertiser**
              Reporter (vacation work) – This was my first experience of working in the
              media, and working as a trainee reporter taught me how to source and tailor
              stories to the specific target audience. It was also my first experience of
              working in a highly pressurised and time-sensitive environment. Three of my
              articles were published.

1998-1999   **Hornbeam House** (Anytown)
              Volunteer – This work involved caring for mentally ill residents and the
              organisation of various therapeutic group activities. The residents were all
              young adults.

1997-1998   **Anytown Social Services**
              Ambulance Guide – The role of this position included care work for severely
              mentally ill patients during transport to and from special care centres. I was
              also actively involved with patient care and the organisation of group
              activities at the centres.

PERSONAL INFORMATION

              At University I was a member of the film-making club and wrote regularly for
              the in-house magazine. I enjoy film and drama, comedy, literature, music and
              most sports, playing at football at weekends. I also enjoy travelling (both this
              country and abroad) and experimenting with vegetarian cookery. I am
              passionate about environmental and conservation issues and do voluntary
              'hands-on' work for the Footpaths and Walkways Association.

REFEREES

              Mr David Davidson, Tutor, University College Anytown,
              The High, Anytown AX1 1AA.
              Telephone: 0111 101 2321.

              Mrs Jocelyn Jones, Director, PNP Promotions,
              PNP House, Grange Drive, Anytown AX1 3ED
              Telephone: 0111 199 5555.

Appendix 3

Sample letters of application

Remember that the letter of application introduces you to the recruiter (through your CV). It is the first thing the recruiter looks at and first impressions are critical. If your letter does not catch the eye of the recruiter, your CV may not even be read.

Here are some ways of creating 'letter appeal':

● formal (not casual) writing;
● sensible styling and neatness;
● good grammar and spelling;
● concise and clear content;
● addressed properly (correct name and job title);
● good construction – a beginning, middle and end;
● print on the best quality paper you can;
● use short confident phrases and sentences;
● words should be strong, positive and confident (refer to the lists of key words in Step 2: Your personal sales 'tool kit');
● avoid jargon, abbreviations and words not in common usage;
● if relevant, identify the source of the advertisement or contact;
● personalize the letter by highlighting relevant experience or achievements specified.

The templates of letters that follow are provided for guidance and can be used as a base to work from.

Speculative letter (cold call)

Letterhead, covering:
Your address and telephone number (include your name if you wish)

Date

I Select Esq
Personnel Manager
AnyCo Limited
200 Commercial Road
Anytown
AA1 1AA

Dear Mr Select

My research into your Company indicates that you may be recruiting graduates in the summer for full time positions. I was particularly interested in the product information on your web site and the statements you make about your ambitions and goals which I find attractive and exciting.

Rather than waiting for the graduate recruitment fairs and advertisements I am approaching you now as I believe that I have the educational background and qualities that you may be looking for. My degree [*or other qualification*] is in _____ and I am predicted to get a _____ [*grade*]. I am enthusiastic by nature and thrive on responsibility and teamwork, I am willing to learn and have excellent communication skills together with a good sense of humour.

I enclose my CV for your information and would welcome the chance to meet you and discuss possible opportunities.

Yours sincerely

[*Signature space*]

Print your name

Response to advertisement

Letterhead, covering:
Your address and telephone number (include your name if you wish)

Date

I. Select Esq
Personnel Manager
AnyCo Limited
200 Commercial Road
Anytown
AA1 1AA

Dear Mr Select

Graduate Trainee

I refer to your advertisement for a Graduate Trainee, which appeared in the 'Anytime Gazette' of 21 February 2____. Having now had the opportunity to research your company on the Internet I believe that it is an organization I should like to join and one that would best use my talents.

My interests lie in the field of _____, and I will complete my course at _____ College in June ____, where I am predicted to achieve a _____ [*degree or other qualification*] in _____ [*subject*]. In my final year my project has been based on _____ and my dissertation explored _____, which I refer to in my CV. I am enthusiastic by nature and thrive on responsibility and teamwork. I am willing to learn and have excellent communication skills together with a good sense of humour.

I enclose my CV for your information and would welcome the chance to meet you and discuss possible opportunities.

Yours sincerely

[*Signature space*]

Print your name

Appendix 4

Forms for photocopying

The forms on the following pages may be photocopied for your personal use. These forms can also be downloaded from the companion website at www.careerskills.org.uk. We hope you will find them useful or that they will help you design your own – the objective is to ensure that you keep control of your job search.

The harder I practise the luckier I get.

Gary Player
(South African professional golfer)

Websites – career choices/job search*

delete as appropriate.

List website addresses you have found which give access to good career choice information or assist with your job search (as appropriate)	Note information gained, for future reference – detail careers researched, etc. Cross-reference job searches with the Job search campaign – control sheet

Experiences catalogue form

Events or experiences	Analysis of the experience
List all the events that have occurred in your life so far – from school, college, university, home life, leisure or working time. Then highlight those that you feel are noteworthy.	For each highlighted experience, answer the question: 'What have I gained from that event or experience; how has it helped me develop as a person, or what lessons have I learnt?'

Self-audit form

My strengths, abilities and skills	Areas I need to develop
Answer the question: 'What am I good at, what are my strengths and abilities?' Take a few minutes and write down everything you can think of. Don't be modest or undervalue yourself.	Now answer the question: 'What do I need to improve, what areas of my make-up need working on?' Be realistic, but not too hard on yourself.

Copy this form and ask a trusted friend, relative, etc., to answer the questions for you, and compare the results. Add to your form later as more ideas come to you. Keep the completed form for future reference to compare your progress and improvement in all areas.

Networking control sheet

Contact name	Telephone, fax, email details	Contact code*	Introduced by**	Details of approach/request	Outcome of approach	Follow up†

Note: * Contact codes   1. Known to you personally; 2. Met (introduced by a friend); 3. Not met (friend recommended approach).

** Details if not directly known to you.

† If the contact comes from a network contact remember to advise them of the outcome of the approach and thank them for their help.

Job search campaign – control sheet

Organization name and address	Telephone, fax, email details	Contact name	Source	Vacancy	Dates of contact	Interview Yes/No	Comments/outcome

Note: If your source comes from your network, remember to advise your contact of the outcome of the approach and thank them for their introduction and help.

Interview assessment form

Complete this form as soon as possible after your interview (be honest!).

Company/organization:	
Location:	Date:
Name of interviewer/s:	

Was I on time?	**Yes / No**	Was I confident?	**Yes / No**
Were my answers clear?	**Yes / No**	Was I relaxed?	**Yes / No**
Was I enthusiastic?	**Yes / No**	Was eye contact good (not staring)?	**Yes / No**
Did I speak clearly (not gabble)?	**Yes / No**	Did I waffle?	**Yes / No**
Was my posture good?	**Yes / No**	Was I well mannered?	**Yes / No**
Did I sound coherent?	**Yes / No**	Did I fidget?	**Yes / No**

What did I do well?

Tricky questions:

Was my research good enough? If not, why?

Anything I could have done better?

Ideas for the next interview:

Overall:

Did I enjoy the interview?	**Yes / No**	Did I do my best?	**Yes / No**

What happens next?

CV working paper

Use this form in conjunction with the notes in Step 2: Your personal sales 'tool kit' to prepare your CV.

Personal details

Educational records School, college, university – dates attended; examination levels and passes; special-interest items

Work records Include vacational work (group repeated jobs together), voluntary or social activities

CV working paper (continued)

Special skills
Skills and aptitudes that you have developed, including any which may have relevance to the work environment, such as computer literacy (giving an indication of the level of your ability)

Other interests
Hobbies, interests, pastimes etc., especially if they involve social or community activities. Highlight any which show you taking responsibility

Profile
The aim is to describe yourself in a punchy, positive, factual manner – highlight areas of strength (refer to your Self-audit form). This important part of your CV is aimed at 'grabbing' the interviewer's attention. The positive descriptions in the Key word lists in Step 2 (p. 13) may be of some help.

Index